CALVINISM

AND THE

Southern Baptist Convention

A Response to Non-Calvinist Objections

Rodney S. Walls

Ichthus Publications · Apollo, Pennsylvania

SPECIAL THANKS

There are some people to whom I wish to say a special "thank you."

First, I have been thinking and learning about the doctrines of grace for nearly three decades now. During that time, I have had many teachers, both ancient and contemporary. I am deeply indebted to all of them, but perhaps to the late R. C. Sproul more than anyone else.

Second, I want to thank Ichthus Publications for taking a chance on an unpublished author like me. When I first began to explore how to get a manuscript published, I was told by one author that it was very difficult to "break through." He said his first book remained in his computer for nearly ten years before he finally found a publisher. So, I am humbled and profoundly grateful for this incredible Providence.

Third, I would like to thank my editor, Adam Murrell, for believing in this project and for your invaluable contribution to it. Thank you for your gracious spirit. You have been a joy to work with.

Fourth, I must thank my dear friends and fellow-pastors: Eric Boyd, Ryan Millar, Greg Nash, and Derek Paul. Thank you for encouraging me to write this book. Because of your collective wisdom, what was initially going to be an open letter was converted into book form and adapted for the general reader. Thanks also for your feedback through conversations, emails, texts, and editing. Derek, I am especially grateful for the many hours you spent searching for typos in those early editions of the manuscript!

Fifth, I want to thank Ms. Ruth McNeese for offering a fresh set of eyes on the manuscript before it went to the press. You have an exceptional gift with editing. I am honored to have you as my friend!

Sixth, special thanks always and forever to my wife, Pamela Walls, for never failing to believe in me. Even if the whole world stood against me, I know who would be standing right there by my side. We truly are partners in life, in love, and in ministry. And I am eternally grateful to God for you!

Finally, and most of all, I want to thank my Lord and Savior Jesus Christ, to whose glory and honor I dedicated my labors for this little book. As I was in the process of writing it, I prayed that if You allowed it to be published, all the proceeds would be given to support missions through the International Mission Board, affiliated with the Southern Baptist Convention. You have answered my prayers, and I will most gladly honor my promise.

Soli Deo Gloria!

Contents

Introduction

A Personal Story

I remember well my first encounter with the doctrine of divine election. I was twenty-one years old and a junior in college. I was alone in my one-bedroom apartment, reading my Bible, as I was in the habit of doing every morning. It just so happened that I was reading Romans 9, a text that I had read many times before. But this particular morning I saw something in verses 10–13 that apparently I had missed in previous readings:

> And not only so, but also when Rebekah had conceived children by one man, our forefather Isaac, though they were not yet born and had done nothing either good or bad—in order that God's purpose of election might continue, not because of works but because of him who calls—she was told, "The older will serve the younger." As it is written, "Jacob I loved, but Esau I hated."

Say *what*?

I paused for a moment and continued reading in verses 14–20:

> What shall we say then? Is there injustice on God's part? By no means! For he says to Moses, "I will have mercy on whom I have mercy, and I will have compassion on whom I have compassion." So then it depends not on human will or exertion, but on God, who has mercy. For the Scripture says to Pharaoh, "For this very purpose I have raised you up, that I might show my power in you, and that my name might be proclaimed in all the earth." So then he has mercy on whomever he wills, and he hardens whomever he wills. You will say to me then, "Why does he still find fault? For who can resist his will?" But who are you, O man, to answer back to God? Will what is molded say to its molder, "Why have you made me like this?"

I remember my reaction well. I literally said aloud, "This *can't* be saying what I think it's saying!" I read it through several more times trying to make sense of it. I could not reconcile my understanding of salvation with what was clearly stated in the text. Quite frankly, it was *disturbing*.

What Is Calvinism?

I went to see my pastor to discuss with him this passage from Romans 9. It was a brief discussion. He articulated to me that Paul was *not* saying what I thought he was saying. He assured me that God is a just God and that He does not make decisions arbitrarily. God's choice of us for salvation is based on His foreknowledge of our freewill response to Jesus. God knows ahead of time whether we will choose Christ or reject Christ and, based on the choice we will make, God then chooses or rejects us. At the time, I felt ill-equipped to reply, but I was not at all satisfied with his interpretation. Nevertheless, out of respect for him, I did not openly disagree. And I never brought the subject up to him again.

This was the beginning of a long and arduous theological struggle for me. My questions only grew more intense with time. Several years would pass before I fully embraced what is commonly referred to as *Calvinism*. Before this, however, I read the works and listened to sermons of both Calvinists and non-Calvinists alike. Indeed, for some time I lived in limbo, vacillating between both camps, yet never fully embracing either.

Those days are long gone now and today I am unashamedly a Calvinist. But I share my story to let the reader know that I understand what it is to wrestle with this subject. I understand many of the objections to Calvinism raised by non-Calvinists. And it is primarily to non-Calvinists that I write—especially if you are a Southern Baptist.

The Purpose of This Book

You see, in recent decades Calvinism has become increasingly controversial within the Southern Baptist Convention (SBC). This is truly sad given the fact that Calvinism is the heritage of the SBC.[1] Many today are confused about what Calvinism teaches. Unfortunately, some non-Calvinist SBC leaders only add to the confusion with their misrepresentations of Calvinism. This book is an attempt to clear up some of that confusion by answering some of the more popular objections to Calvinism raised by non-Calvinists. So I invite my non-Calvinist brothers and sisters in the Lord to read with an open mind and heart. Of course, I will try to persuade you with my arguments, and I hope that you will even come to embrace the doctrines of grace.[2] But even if you do not agree with my theology, I hope that once you have read the book you will have been stretched to think about some things that perhaps you have never before considered. And I trust that you will have gained a much better understanding of what Calvinism actually teaches.

This book is written primarily for laypeople who have serious questions about Calvinism, but who have little or no theological training. That does not mean this is an easy read. If you have an interest in

---

[1] This Calvinistic heritage will be demonstrated in chapter 2.
[2] The terms *Calvinism*, *Reformed theology*, and the *doctrines of grace* will be discussed in chapter 1.

this subject at all, then you probably already know that we are not dealing with cake-and-ice cream here. This is meat-and-potatoes kind of stuff. You will need to put on your thinking cap. But I assure you that my writing style is very lay-friendly. You should be able to follow my train of thought even if you disagree with my arguments. You may find some of the footnotes a little more challenging. However, rather than a burden to wade through, I think you will find the footnotes extremely helpful. In fact, the footnotes are "gold" if you are willing to dig for it. Some readers may find it easier to read the text through first and then come back to the footnotes afterwards.

This book is also written for non-Calvinist SBC pastors and other leaders who may have *some* knowledge of Calvinism, but not enough. Over the years, I have encountered many such leaders who *think* they understand Calvinism, but who actually do not. They understand *some* things correctly, and yet they have a very distorted understanding of other things. To be sure, much of the confusion about Calvinism in the SBC today is due in large part to the misunderstandings of many non-Calvinist leaders who feel compelled to warn their congregations and Baptist associations about the "dangers" of Calvinism. Of all people, Christian leaders should take the greatest care to articulate theology as accurately as possible—even that of their opponents! Concern for truth and close attention to accuracy is imperative, or legitimate critique that may be warranted will carry no weight.

Of course, Calvinist pastors may find this book a useful tool to place into the hands of non-Calvinists who have questions about Calvinism.

I offer this book as a labor of love to my denominational family, the SBC—and especially to my non-Calvinist brothers and sisters in Jesus Christ. May the Lord use it to help you work through some of your questions and concerns about Calvinism and to gain a better understanding of what Calvinism teaches.

Rodney S. Walls

I

What Is Calvinism?

Calvinism and Reformed Theology

Many people use the terms *Calvinism* and *Reformed theology* interchangeably. Technically speaking, however, there are subtle differences between the two terms. Essentially, *Reformed theology* is broader in scope and deals not just with the doctrine of salvation, but with matters pertaining to church polity, worship, etc. *Calvinism* pertains specifically to salvation and is thus a subset of historic Reformed theology. But again, the terms *Calvinism* and *Reformed theology* are often used interchangeably, and perhaps we should not make too much of this distinction. Furthermore, both terms are used synonymously with the moniker *doctrines of grace*, which pertain specifically to salvation. And yet, both terms are also used in reference to a particular worldview that emphasizes God's absolute sovereignty over *all* things, not just the salvation of sinners. Consequently, Jim Orrick is surely right when he asserts:

> Calvinism is more than the Five Points. Before we can make any significant progress toward determining the truthfulness of the Five Points, we need to understand that God always does as he pleases. . . . Calvinism is a way of looking at the world. It is a way of thinking about everything. The Calvinistic way of thinking is rooted in the confidence that God is in control of everything and everyone and that he is controlling everything according to his good and perfect purpose.[1]

The Doctrines of Grace and TULIP

As previously stated, Calvinism is a nickname for the term *doctrines of grace* (otherwise known as the *five points* of Calvinism). These doctrines have often been formulated with the acronym *TULIP*. We will discuss these in more detail in the following chapters. Below is a summary of each doctrine.

T = *total depravity* (or radical corruption): Man

---

[1] Jim Scott Orrick, *Mere Calvinism*, (Phillipsburg, NJ: P&R Publishing, 2019), 17, 23. Likewise, R. C. Sproul claims: "Reformed theology is first and foremost theocentric rather than anthropocentric. That is, it is God-centered rather than man-centered. . . . In Reformed theology, if God is not sovereign over the entire created order, then he is not sovereign at all. The term *sovereignty* too easily becomes a chimera. If God is not sovereign, then he is not God. It belongs to God as God to be sovereign." R. C. Sproul, *What Is Reformed Theology? Understanding the Basics* (Grand Rapids, MI: Baker Books, 1997), 25, 27.

has a depraved nature. Man is not *utterly* depraved; that is, he is not as wicked as he can possibly be. But he is *radically* depraved in that every aspect of his being (mind, affections, will, body) has been corrupted by sin. He is spiritually dead in sin and therefore does not have the ability either to seek God by his own initiative or turn to Him in faith for salvation.

U = *unconditional election*: From all eternity God decided to save certain individuals from the mass of humanity and pass over the rest. God's choice is *unconditional*—it is not based upon any foreseen human merit or decision. God does not look down the corridors of time to see who will respond to the gospel and then choose us based upon our decision. God's choice of us for salvation precedes our choice of Him. God's decision is not arbitrary but rather is in accordance with His own sovereign pleasure and purpose. There is no *injustice* in God's sovereign choice. The elect receive *mercy*; the non-elect receive *justice*.

L = *limited atonement* (or definite atonement): God did not send His Son into the world to make redemption merely *possible* for everyone; rather, God's intent was to make salvation *certain* for the elect. Christ laid down His life *for His sheep*. Christ's death atoned for the sins of a *definite* number, a *particular* people, the elect of God.

I = *irresistible grace* (or effectual calling): Those

whom God has elected unto salvation He *effectively calls* and regenerates. That is, when God *effectually calls* spiritually dead sinners to salvation, He quickens (regenerates) them via an inward operation on the soul. In so doing, God overcomes the sinner's natural inclination to resist His saving grace by taking away "the heart of stone" and giving us "a heart of flesh" (Ezek. 11:19; 36:26). He thereby changes the disposition of the heart which is bent on self and sin and gives us a desire for Christ and for the things of God. No one is ever saved by divine coercion. No one is ever saved against his or her will.

P = *perseverance of the saints* (or preservation of the saints): All whom God elects unto salvation He *preserves* by His sustaining grace until the end of their lives. To be sure, believers are called upon to *persevere* in their faith unto the end, but the primary reason they succeed in doing so is because God *preserves* them by His grace.

John Calvin Did *Not* Invent Calvinism

Many falsely assume that these doctrines came directly from John Calvin. Not only that, but many also think that Calvin was obsessed with the doctrine of *predestination*. To the contrary, as Timothy George fittingly recognizes, although "predestination was a fact of Scripture," for Calvin, it was "not the controlling principle of all Christian doctrine."[2] Calvin, in fact, used a great deal of discretion in his handling of the doctrine of predestination. According to R. C. Sproul, an expert on Protestant Reformation theology, "Calvin wrote sparingly on the subject." Indeed, as Sproul further notes, the German Reformer, Martin Luther, "wrote far more about predestination than did Calvin."[3]

No, John Calvin did not invent Calvinism. As James Boice and Philip Ryken observe:

> Although these doctrines constitute the purest expression of Calvinism, Calvin did not invent them, nor were they characteristic of his thought alone during the Reformation period. These truths are contained in the Old Testament Psalms. They were taught by Jesus, even to his enemies, as recorded in John 6 and 10 and elsewhere. The apostle Paul confirmed them in his letters to the Romans, the Ephesians, and others. . . . Martin Luther was in many ways a Calvinist . . . So were Ulrich Zwingli and William Tyndale. For this reason, it is perhaps more accurate to describe this theology as "Reformational" rather than "Calvinist."[4]

---

[2] Timothy George, *Amazing Grace: God's Pursuit, Our Response*, Second Edition (Wheaton, IL: Crossway, 2011), 71.

[3] R. C. Sproul, *Chosen By God* (Carol Stream, IL: Tyndale House, 1986), 15.

[4] James Montgomery Boice and Philip Graham Ryken, *The Doctrines of*

Furthermore, the "five points" were not even formulated until nearly half a century after Calvin's death. They were devised in response to the five points of Jacob Arminius' followers, who were known as the Remonstrants because they protested, or *remonstrated*, against Reformed theology. The Remonstrants were condemned at the Synod of Dort (1618–1619) in Dordrecht, the Netherlands, and the five points of orthodox Reformed theology were affirmed.[5]

Troubled by TULIP

According to Kenneth Stewart, there is no evidence of the acronym TULIP being used before the twentieth century.[6] Indeed, many Calvinists are uncomfortable with this acronym. As Stewart notes: "The doctrines summarized under the rubric of TULIP are capable of being grossly misunderstood. (Total depravity, limited atonement and irresistible grace are

---

Grace: Rediscovering the Evangelical Gospel, (Wheaton, IL: Crossway Books, 2002), 19. Michael Horton attests: "Before the Reformation, there were many respected theologians who defended these doctrines under the nickname 'Augustinian.' Besides Augustine himself, we think of Anselm, Gregory of Rimini, Archbishop Bradwardine, and Luther's own mentor, Johann von Staupitz, who led the Augustinian order in Germany and wrote a marvelous tract defending these truths even before Luther." Michael Horton, *For Calvinism* (Grand Rapids, MI: Zondervan, 2011), 19.

[5] See Boice and Ryken, *The Doctrines of Grace*, 18, 24–33; see also Horton, *For Calvinism*, 19–21.

[6] Kenneth J. Stewart, *Ten Myths About Calvinism: Rediscovering the Breadth of the Reformed Tradition*, (Downers Grove, IL: InterVarsity, 2011), 75–96.

the items most often admitted to be problematic)."[7]

Because the terms *Calvinism* and *Reformed theology* are so often mischaracterized today, I prefer to speak of the *doctrines of grace*. Nevertheless, in the following chapters I will use the terms *Calvinism*, *Reformed theology* and *the doctrines of grace* interchangeably.

Calvinism is the Gospel

Before we conclude this chapter, we do well to consider how one famous English Baptist preacher used the term *Calvinism* in his day (mid to late 1800s). Charles H. Spurgeon stated:

> We only use the term "Calvinism" for shortness. That doctrine which is called "Calvinism" did not spring from Calvin; we believe that it sprang from the great founder of all truth. . . . We use the term then, not because we impute an extraordinary importance to Calvin's having taught these doctrines. We would be just as willing to call them by any other name, if we could be as consistent with the fact.[8]

---

[7] Ibid., 77. George argues: "It would be better if we could stop talking about 'points' at all! In a certain sense, there is only one point—the God of grace and glory. In another sense, there are at least sixty-six points, since every book in the Bible sets forth the gospel of grace" (*Amazing Grace*, 83).

[8] Cited in Robert B. Selph, *Southern Baptists and the Doctrine of Election* (Harrisonburg, VA: Sprinkle Publications, 1988), 62. Ernest C. Reisinger, Publisher's Introduction to J. P. Boyce's *Abstract of Systematic Theology*,

But what exactly did Spurgeon mean by the term *Calvinism*? Was he a so-called "moderate" Calvinist, like many in our day?[9] Spurgeon himself cleared up any confusion about the matter when he stated:

> There is no such thing as preaching Christ and Him crucified, unless you preach what is now-a-days called Calvinism. . . . It is a nickname to call it Calvinism; *Calvinism is the gospel*, and nothing else.[10] I do not believe we preach the gospel, if we do not preach justification by faith without works; not unless we preach the sovereignty of God in his dispensation of grace; not unless we exalt the electing, unchangeable, eternal, immutable, conquering love of Jehovah; nor do I think we can preach the gospel, unless we base it upon the

Reprinted Edition (Pompano Beach, FL: Christian Gospel Foundation, original copy 1887), XXI. The great evangelist George Whitefield said: "I embrace the Calvinistic scheme, not because Calvin, but Jesus Christ has taught it to me." Arnold Dallimore, *George Whitefield*, Vol. 1 (Edinburgh, UK: Banner of Truth Trust, 1970), 406.

[9] I have long been puzzled by the label *"moderate Calvinist."* Ironically, some people identify themselves by this term while holding to only one out of the five points of Calvinism (the doctrine of *the perseverance of the saints*). One cannot help but wonder why such people would want to identify with *Calvinism* at all. Nevertheless, many do, all the while despising John Calvin himself!

[10] Commenting on this statement, Horton explains: "At first blush, Spurgeon's comment sounds sectarian. Clearly, he did not mean that only Calvinists believe and proclaim the gospel—in fact, throughout his public ministry he expressed respect for evangelical Arminians like John Wesley. His point was that the doctrines of grace, which for better or worse are nicknamed 'Calvinism,' are not really Calvin's, but the teaching of the Scriptures, Augustine, and a trail of preachers, reformers, missionaries, and evangelists ever since" (*For Calvinism*, 19).

peculiar redemption which Christ made for his elect and chosen people; nor can I comprehend a gospel which lets saints fall away after they are called (emphasis mine).[11]

Clearly, C. H. Spurgeon, perhaps the greatest Baptist preacher of all time (as reputation would have it), was an unapologetic, five-point Calvinist!

---

[11] Cited in Selph, *Southern Baptists and the Doctrine of Election*, 65. Arthur Custance, *The Sovereignty of Grace* (Phillipsburg, NJ: P&R Publishing, 1979), 135–136.

2

Calvinism and the SBC?

Did you know that the heritage of the SBC is staunchly and overwhelmingly *Calvinistic*? The SBC was organized in Augusta, Georgia in 1845. The founders, without exception, were historic, orthodox Calvinists. According to Timothy George:

> Each of the 293 "delegates," as they were then called, who gathered in Augusta to organize the Southern Baptist Convention . . . in 1845, belonged to congregations and associations which had adopted the Philadelphia/Charleston Confession of Faith as their own.[1]

---

[1] Timothy George, *Baptist Confessions, Covenants, and Catechisms*, eds. Timothy and Denise George (Nashville, TN: Broadman and Holman, 1996), 11.

The Second London Confession

The *Philadelphia/Charleston Confession of Faith* is a slightly revised version of the 1689 *Baptist Confession of Faith*, also known as the *Second London Confession (SLC)*. Let us get a little background on this.

First, Baptists have been around now for just a little over four hundred years. Very early in our history two branches formed: the General Baptists and the Particular Baptists, the primary difference being over their understanding of salvation. The General Baptists believed in a "general atonement," that Christ died for people in *general* and therefore His death atoned for the sins of the whole world, for every individual person. The Particular Baptists, conversely, believed in a "limited atonement" or a "particular redemption," that Christ died for a *particular* people, God's elect. We will examine this issue in more detail in chapter 4.

Second, according to the legendary Baptist historian, Tom Nettles:

> The *Second London Confession*, adopted by Particular Baptists in England in 1677, followed very closely the *Westminster Confession of Faith* [WCF], but differed significantly in ecclesiology, ordinances, and the relationship of the church and state.[2]

[2] Thomas J. Nettles, *By His Grace and for His Glory: A Historical, Theo-*

Other than that, however, the *SLC* and the *WCF* are virtually identical. The doctrines of grace are unmistakably delineated and promoted in both confessions.

Third, when the Particular Baptists left England for America, they brought the *SLC* with them. In America the *SLC* became known as the *Philadelphia Confession of Faith* (1742). In the South it became known as the *Charleston Confession of Faith* (1767), which formed the basis for the *Abstract of Principles*, which was adopted in 1858 as the guiding confessional statement for The Southern Baptist Theological Seminary.

So that's the background behind the *Philadelphia/ Charleston Confession of Faith*. Consequently, the 293 delegates who met in 1845 to organize the SBC were steeped in the historic Calvinist tradition.[3]

Calvinism in the Antebellum South

Commenting on what the antebellum Baptist historian David Benedict saw in his own day, Nettles writes:

A much greater influence of the doctrines of

logical and Practical Study of the Doctrines of Grace in Baptist Life, Revised and Expanded 20th Anniversary Edition (Cape Coral, FL: Founders Press, 2006), xii.

[3] Nettles observes: "Calvinism was the dominant theology in the most enduring areas of Baptist life for the first 275 years of modern Baptist history. Its energy generated the establishment of churches, the missionary enterprise, and the agencies and institutions of Baptist life" (Ibid., 466).

grace persisted in the South than in the New England states. [Benedict] saw that the *Philadelphia Confession of Faith* was especially influential in the middle and southern states and that the doctrines of "depravity, election, divine sovereignty, final perseverance, etc., were enforced strongly further south."[4]

That being the case, let us narrow our scope a bit and focus on Georgia Baptists, bearing in mind that what occurred there is representative of Baptist life throughout the antebellum South.

According to Greg Wills, Professor of Church History at The Southern Baptist Theological Seminary, the *SLC* was the standard confession for early Georgia Baptists. Wills observes: "Some associations praised the London Confession and formulated their creed as a synopsis of the longer confession. . . . A small number of southern associations adopted the London Confession itself."[5] The Sarepta Baptist Association (SBA) was established in 1799 and is one of the oldest associations in the state of Georgia. Printed below are Articles 3, 4, and 6 of the Constitution of the SBA for the years of 1799 through 1849:

3. We believe in the fall of Adam, and the im-

---

[4] Ibid., 107. David Benedict, *A General History of the Baptist Denomination in America* (New York, NY: Lewis Colby & Co., 1853), 137.

[5] Gregory A. Wills, *Democratic Religion: Freedom, Authority, and Church Discipline in the Baptist South 1785-1900* (New York, NY: Oxford, 1997), 104–05, 171.

putation of his sin to his posterity; In the corruption of human nature and the impotency
of man to recover himself by his own free will
or ability.

4. We believe in the everlasting love of God to
his people and the eternal election of a definite number of the human race to grace and
glory: and that there was a covenant of grace
or redemption made between the Father and
the Son before the world began in which their
salvation is secure, and that they in particular
are redeemed.

6. We believe that all those who were chosen
in Christ, will be effectually called, regenerated, converted, sanctified and supported by the
spirit and power of God, so that they shall
persevere in grace, and not one of them be finally lost.[6]

These articles clearly affirm the *doctrines of
grace*. Article 3 affirms *total depravity*; Article 4, *unconditional election* and *definite atonement*; and Article 6, *effectual calling* and *the preservation of the
saints*.

Moreover, in his magisterial study of nineteenth-

---

[6] The History Committee Sarepta Baptist Association, *Minutes of the
Sarepta Baptist Association For the Years of 1799 Through 1849*, Restored
from the Micro-Film of Minutes and from the printed Minutes for these
years (Athens, GA: Sarepta Baptist Association, 2002), pp 2–3.

century Georgia Baptists, Greg Wills confirms this Calvinistic heritage when he writes:

> Despite pockets of Arminian or freewill sentiment among Baptists in the South, few southern Baptists embraced Arminianism before the twentieth century. . . . By 1846, Arminian Baptists numbered almost 2,000, but accounted for only 3 percent of Georgia's 58,000 Baptists. By 1870, of some 115,000 Georgia Baptists, only 808 were members of Arminian churches. Late into the nineteenth century, pastors could still expect the approbation of their colleagues for boasting that their church was "perfectly sound in doctrine, especially Calvinistic."[7] . . . The most visible display of Baptist Calvinism appeared in the confessions of faith adopted by Baptist churches and associations. Virtually every church creed affirmed the two fundamental tenets of Calvinism: that human nature was radically depraved due to original sin and that God was the absolute author of salvation, electing individuals for salvation before the creation of the world and creating faith by the operation of the Holy Spirit. . . . Regular southern Baptists would not maintain fellow-

[7] J. M. Stillwell, "Social Circle, Stone Mountain, Indian Creek," *The Christian Index*, 27 November 1873, 2. See *Minutes*, Georgia Baptist Convention, 1846, 27; "Statistical Table of the Denomination in Georgia," in *Minutes*, Georgia Baptist Convention.

ship with Arminian churches, or approve the sending of letters or visitors to Arminian churches. . . . The Chattahoochee Association instructed churches to defrock any minister "who publicly denounces the doctrine of human depravity, Salvation by grace, and makes general war on the doctrine of Election."[8] The Sarepta Association told them to refuse church office even to anyone who did not "believe it to be expedient to preach and contend for the doctrine of predestination and election."[9] One after another, associations counseled their churches to expel any preachers who taught "that Christ atoned for the whole human family," denied a "special, and eternal election,"[10] or refused to proclaim "the doctrine of Election."[11] They advised them to punish laity who dared suggest "that Christ died indiscriminately for all men."[12] The Tugalo Association said that believers baptized by "free will"[13] preachers had to be baptized again. As late as 1891, Baptist leaders argued that "an applicant for admission [to church membership] who rejects the doctrine of election should not be admitted."[14]

[8] Manuscript minutes, Chattahoochee Baptist Association, 1871, 76, MU.
[9] Manuscript minutes, Sarepta Baptist Association, 1830, 123.
[10] *Minutes*, Flint River Baptist Association, 1829, 2.
[11] Manuscript minutes, Tugalo Baptist Association, 1824, 23.
[12] *Minutes*, Western Baptist Association, 1833, 5–6.
[13] Manuscript minutes, Tugalo Baptist Association, 1831, 52.
[14] I. R. Branham, "More Samples," *The Christian Index*, October 1891, 8.

For most nineteenth-century southern Baptists, to reject Calvinism was to deny the gospel of grace. . . . From one corner of the state to another, churches and associations defrocked preachers for questioning Calvinist doctrines, criticized even slight alterations in Calvinist creeds, and blocked fellowship with doctrinally careless congregations.[15]

Calvinism *is* the heritage of the SBC. And for the first eighty years of the SBC's history, this was the predominant theology.[16]

---

[15] Wills, *Democratic Religion*, 103, 106, 108. Regarding the Sarepta Baptist Association, one extremely influential Georgia Baptist, Patrick H. Mell, served two terms as the president of the SBC (1863–1871; 1880–1887) and even served for a while as chancellor of the University of Georgia (1878–1888). Mell's influence in the Athens region was extensive. He served for twenty-five years as the pastor of Antioch Baptist Church (ABC) located in Oglethorpe County. According to Wills: "Mell . . . 'took charge in 1852' and concluded that 'a number of members were drifting into Arminianism.' Mell decided that a Baptist church should have Baptist doctrine, and therefore he 'preached to them the doctrines of predestination, election, free-grace.' So popular was his Calvinist preaching during his twenty-five year pastorate that a Methodist preacher called the region 'Mell's Kingdom'" (*Democratic Religion*, 107–108). Moreover, the Georgia Baptist pastor Samuel Boykin said of Mell: "On the doctrines of Christianity and especially the (so called) 'five points' in theology, he is especially able." Samuel Boykin, *History of the Baptist Denomination in Georgia* (Atlanta, GA: The Christian Index, 1881), 382. Incidentally, during his twenty-five year pastorate at ABC, Mell also served for a short time (1868–1869) as the pastor of Lexington Baptist Church (LBC)—also located in Oglethorpe county—where I was privileged to serve as pastor from 2010– 2015. In fact, LBC was established in 1847 by some of the members of ABC.

[16] Robert Selph claims: "Perhaps the Southern Baptist attitude toward the doctrines of grace in the first eighty years finds its most succinct summary in a letter written by John A. Broadus from Europe about his impressions in Geneva [where Calvin ministered]: 'The people who sneer at what is called Calvinism might as well sneer at Mount Blanc. We are not in the least bound to defend all of Calvin's opinions or actions, but I do not see how

Calvinism in the Modern Era

Throughout the twentieth century, Southern Baptists drifted far from their roots as Calvinism waned from about 1920 until around 1980. Since that time, there has been a resurgence of Calvinism within the SBC, which has alarmed many non-Calvinist SBC leaders. So much so that if an SBC pastor embraces the doctrines of grace today, he may very well be branded an "extremist," or perhaps even a "heretic."[17]

In 2012, Dr. Gerald Harris, current editor of *The Christian Index*, wrote an article titled "The Calvinists Are Here."[18] It caused no little stir in the state of Georgia (and beyond). "Sound the alarm! Blow the trumpet! Beware! The Calvinists are here!" But as has been clearly demonstrated, the Calvinists have

anyone who really understands the Greek of the Apostle Paul or the Latin of Calvin or Turretin can fail to see that the latter did but interpret and formulate substantially what the former teaches'" (*Southern Baptists and the Doctrine of Election*, 62). Quotation from Thomas J. Nettles, *Baptist Catechisms*, ed. Thomas J. Nettles (Memphis, TN: Mid-America Baptist Seminary), 227.

[17] I once preached a sermon on unconditional election. Afterwards, a retired SBC pastor accused me of teaching *heresy* and said that he could not have fellowship with me unless I repented. Another SBC leader branded me an *extreme Calvinist* because I affirm the doctrines of grace.

[18] This article is available online at https://founders.org/2012/02/10/ georgia-indexs-gerald-harris-on-the-calvinists-are-here/. Ironically, under the editorship of Jesse Mercer and other Georgia Baptist leaders, nineteenth–century subscribers to *The Christian Index* received a steady diet of orthodox Calvinism. According to Wills: "When Samuel Boykin and Sylvanus Landrum took over the [*The Christian Index*], they recommended themselves as 'Calvinistic, strict communion Baptists.' . . . So frequently did the editors write and publish articles on Calvinist theology that a pledge to propagate Calvinism seemed almost prerequisite for holding the editor's chair. As late as 1899, the paper ran a six-month series on Calvinism's 'doctrines of grace'" (*Democratic Religion*, 105).

always been here—and they are not going away.

Nevertheless, concern over Reformed theology's growing influence within the SBC in recent decades has led some SBC leaders to make some rather ridiculous accusations. For example, Pastor Tom Ascol notes that, "In 2012, the 'Statement of the Traditional Southern Baptist Understanding of God's Plan of Salvation' was published by a group of concerned church and denominational leaders in order to assert their doctrinal convictions vis-à-vis the resurgence of the doctrines of grace . . . within the SBC."[19] The following excerpt is taken from the opening paragraph in the preface of this document:

> The precipitating issue for this statement is the rise of a movement called "New Calvinism" among Southern Baptists. This movement is committed to advancing in the churches an exclusively Calvinistic understanding of salvation, characterized by an aggressive insistence on the "Doctrines of Grace" . . . and to the goal of making Calvinism the central Southern Baptist position on God's plan of salvation.[20]

I do not deny that there are some angry Calvinists

[19] Thomas K. Ascol, *Traditional Theology & the SBC: An Interaction and Response to the Traditionalist Statement of God's Plan of Salvation*, Revised Edition (Cape Carol, FL: Founders Press, 2018), 7.

[20] Cited in ibid., 94.

in the SBC. But there are some angry non-Calvinists as well. So when we talk about "an aggressive insistence," it really goes both ways.[21] The real issue, however, is not Calvinism vs. non-Calvinism—it is a matter of the heart. As Pastor Joe Thorn observes:

> When addressing the issue of "those angry Calvinists" we need to be careful and not make Calvinism the issue. It's not about Calvinism. The negativity, pride, and finger wagging is not about the Doctrines of Grace, but the heart. So, when we see such things coming from Calvinists we should seek to point out that this attitude is actually incompatible with Calvinism.[22]

And I would hope that non-Calvinists share these sentiments.

Unfortunately, there are some angry Calvinists who give Calvinism a bad name. But most of us just want to be true to our convictions and have the freedom to teach the Scriptures accordingly. At the same

[21] Ascol opines: "Words have meaning and are a reflection, Jesus said, of what's in the heart. There is a spectrum of views on Calvinism within the SBC. At one extreme we have Calvinists who would be happy to run all non-Calvinists out of the convention (or at least relegate them to the arena of 'being tolerated'). Their counterparts on the other extreme—the anti-Calvinists—have the same agenda but with their guns aimed, obviously, at Calvinists" (Ibid., 15–16).

[22] Joe Thorn, in an interview with Ed Stetzer, cited in "The Problem of 'Angry Calvinists,'" Justin Taylor, September 16, 2011; available at https://www.thegospelcoalition.org/blogs/justin-taylor/the-problem-of-ang ry-calvinists/.

time, we want to extend that same grace to non-Calvinists within the SBC. And if we are going to coexist, both Calvinists and non-Calvinists alike must extend grace to one another in this way.

Furthermore, it is imperative that we not misrepresent one another's theology. I recently learned that a Georgia Associational Missionary warns pastor search committees of churches in his association about the dangers of "extreme Calvinism." Apparently, the material he uses for his presentations is based on Dr. Norman Geisler's book *Chosen But Free*. In so doing, I am sure this Associational Missionary thinks he is doing his association a great service. My concern, however, is that he is simply stoking fear in the minds of people who are already suspicious of Calvinists. Unfortunately, much of the information he is dispensing grossly misrepresents Calvinism.[23] Indeed, this sort of thing is a great *dis*service, not only to the association he is called to serve, but to the denomination as a whole. As stated in the introduction, of all people, Christian leaders should take the greatest care to articulate theology as accurately as possible—even that of their opponents. Concern for truth and close attention to accuracy is imperative for it honors God who is Truth and shows respect for our fellow man; otherwise, legiti-

---

[23] I managed to obtain a copy of the five-page handout that this Associational Missionary uses for his presentations on "extreme Calvinism." Some of the material accurately represents orthodox Calvinism, but much of it is a gross distortion.

mate critique that may be warranted will carry no weight.

My objective in this chapter was to demonstrate from history that historic, five-point Calvinism is the heritage of the SBC. My objective for the remaining chapters is to address some of the misunderstandings and to answer the major objections many people have about Calvinism.[24] In so doing, I pray the Lord will use this book to help bring about a more harmonious relationship between Calvinists and non-Calvinists within the SBC. We may have our disagreements about the doctrine of salvation, but hopefully we can still work together to spread the gospel of our Lord Jesus Christ, at home and abroad.

May the Lord grant it. Amen.

---

[24] This book is not designed to be an exhaustive treatise and therefore makes no attempt to answer *all* of the objections to Calvinism.

3

Does Man Have Free Will?

Does man have "free will"? It depends on how one defines the term. In this chapter, we will consider both the Calvinistic and non-Calvinistic perspectives on free will. In so doing, we will deal primarily with the Calvinistic doctrines of *total depravity* and *unconditional election*.

Synergism vs. Monergism

Ironically, "moderate" Calvinism has more in common with historic Arminianism than it does with historic Calvinism. For both moderate Calvinism and historic Arminianism have this in common: (1) Both teach that unregenerate man has the ability to choose Christ by his own initiative, and (2) both teach that election is *conditional*, that is, God chooses to save sinners *based on* foreseen faith in them. This is called *synergism*, which means that God's grace cannot save unless man cooperates to some degree with God in his own salvation.[1]

By contrast, Calvinists hold to what is called *monergism*, which means that salvation is wholly the work of the Triune God. The Father decrees salvation, the Son dies to obtain salvation, and the Spirit exercises His power to bring conviction and repentance, leading to salvation. God does not need cooperation with His creatures in order to bring about salvation.[2] Moreover, Calvinists believe that election is *unconditional*. It is not based upon anything inherent *in us* or anything *we do*—including our faith. Rather, election is based upon God's decision alone (Rom. 8:28–39, 9:16; 1 Cor. 1:26–29; Eph. 1:3–14; 2 Thess. 2:13–14; 2 Tim. 1:9–10, etc). As Article V on "Election" in the *Abstract of Principles* states: "Election is God's eternal choice of some persons unto

---

[1] Some contemporary, non-Calvinistic Baptists (who prefer to be called "Traditionalists") are referring to this as *congruent election*. See Richard Land, "Congruent Election: Understanding Election from an 'Eternal Now' Perspective" in *Whosoever Will: A Biblical-Theological Critique of Five-Point Calvinism*, eds. David L. Allen and Steven W. Lemke (Nashville, TN: B&H, 2010), 45–59.

[2] R. C. Sproul explains the difference between these two terms when he writes: "The word *monergism* contains the prefix *mon-*, which means 'one,' and the word *ergon*, which means 'work,' so *monergism* indicates that only one does the work. *Synergism* contains the prefix *syn-*, which means 'with,' so *synergism* has to do with cooperation, with two or more people working together." R. C. Sproul, *Everyone's A Theologian: An Introduction to Systematic Theology* (Sanford, FL: Reformation Trust, 2014), 226. Likewise, Ascol asserts: "Monergism sees regeneration to be a sovereign work of God in which he alone is active—that He gives the new birth without any cooperative effort on the part of the individual. Synergism teaches that God regenerates a person only if and after that person repents and believes" (*Traditional Theology & the* SBC, 53).

everlasting life—*not because of foreseen merit in them*, but of His mere mercy in Christ—in consequence of which choice they are called, justified and glorified" (emphasis added).[3]

True Freedom

According to non-Calvinists, true freedom has to do with choice (between two options) and self-determining power. This is sometimes referred to as *libertarian freedom*. R. C. Sproul explains this position when he states: "Free will is the ability to make choices without any prior prejudice, inclination, or disposition. For the will to be free, it must act from a posture of neutrality, with absolutely no bias."[4] But this will not work. First of all, God is the most free Being there is; indeed, God has *absolute* freedom. And yet God does not act from a posture of neutrality. The *only* prejudices, inclinations, or dispositions God has are to do what is right. God cannot even be tempted to do evil (Jas. 1:13). Second, the saints in heaven are as free to love God as they have ever been or ever will be, and yet the option of choosing against God is impossible.[5] Obviously, this issue is

---

[3] The *Abstract of Principles* is an *abstract* of the 1689 London Baptist Confession of Faith. It was adopted in 1858 as the guiding confessional document for the Southern Baptist Theological Seminary and it is one of the governing documents of Southeastern Baptist Theological Seminary.

[4] Sproul, *Chosen By God*, 51.

[5] Jonathan Edwards, whom many believe to be America's greatest theologian, addressed this argument in his classic book *Freedom of the Will*. Stephen Nichols, an expert on Edwards' theology, summarizes Edwards'

not as simplistic as most non-Calvinists make it out to be.

Many non-Calvinists misunderstand Calvinism to teach that human beings have no free will. But as Article IV on "Providence" in the *Abstract of Principles* asserts, God never "destroy[s] the free will and responsibility of intelligent creatures." So, Calvinists really do believe that human beings have free will, in so far as to say the will freely acts in concert with its nature and acts upon the desires presented to it. What Calvinists deny, however, is that human beings have libertarian freedom.

Total Depravity

So, yes, Calvinists believe that human beings have free will—albeit an enslaved will (John 8:34; Rom. 8:7–8), but it is still a will, nonetheless. It could also rightly be said of humans that we have a "creaturely will." We make decisions every day. We are not, as is oftentimes caricatured of those who believe in the doctrines of grace, robots or puppets. And, to be sure, we make a genuine choice when it comes to the

---

counter-argument to the libertarian freedom position thusly: "Edwards . . . ask[s] . . . When will humanity be most free? He answers that this will be in heaven in the glorified state. He also ponders the question, What being has the most freedom? and answers that it is God. In both ideas he finds an answer to the Arminian view and true meaning of freedom. In both cases freedom has little to do with self-determining power and contingency. Rather, freedom has to do with acting according to one's nature." Stephen J. Nichols, *Jonathan Edwards: A Guided Tour of his Life and Thought* (Phillipsburg, NJ: P&R Publishing, 2001), 180–81.

offer of salvation. The problem is not man's faculty to choose, but rather, his *desire*. It is here, essentially, that the Calvinist view of free will differs from that of the non-Calvinist. Robert Selph explains:

> Man is a creature of choice and has been divinely endowed with a will . . . this is a given. Folks all through the Bible chose to obey God or not to obey God—to receive Jesus or not to receive Him. As we preach and witness to the lost, we appeal, not only to the understanding and affections of men, but also to their wills. . . . They must call upon Him for salvation, and that means they must decide to do it. In this sense, man is a free agent. However, he chooses to do what he *wants* to do. The key problem with man is not his faculty of choice, but his disposition of heart to *desire*. In other words, man left to himself will not choose salvation through Christ on God's terms.[6]

Moreover, Article V on "God's Purpose of Grace" in the *Baptist Faith & Message* (*BF&M*) states that divine election is "consistent with the free agency of

---

[6] Selph, *Southern Baptists and the Doctrine of Election*, 86–87. R. C. Sproul attests: "In the Reformed view of predestination God's choice precedes man's choice. We choose him only because he first chose us. Without divine predestination and without the divine inward call, the Reformed view holds that nobody would ever choose Christ" (*Chosen By God*, 137). We will deal with "the divine inward call" in chapter 5.

man." However, as Selph further declares: "This does not mean . . . that man's will is sovereign and so powerful as to cast the ultimate and deciding vote as to whether he will be saved or not."[7] The reason for this is because, due to the Fall, the will is radically corrupted.[8] Scripture presents us with a bleak picture of fallen humanity. Selph summarizes:

> Every human being by nature is spiritually dead (Ephesians 2:1; Romans 5:12), blind (Ephesians 4:18), defiled in conscience (Titus 1:15–16), trapped in darkness (Colossians 1:13), without understanding (1 Corinthians 2:14), enslaved to sin (John 8:34), hostile toward God (Romans 8:7), a hater of the light (John 3:19–20), without desire for God (Romans 3:11), and without fear of God (Romans 3:18).[9]

---

[7] Ibid., 86.

[8] This is the doctrine of *total (or radical) depravity*, which Michael Horton explains this way: "The 'total' in total depravity refers to its extensiveness, not intensiveness: that is, to the all-encompassing scope of our fallenness. It does not mean that we are as bad as we can possibly be, but that we are all guilty and corrupt to such an extent that there is no hope of pulling ourselves together, brushing ourselves off, and striving (with the help of grace) to overcome God's judgment and our own rebellion" (*For Calvinism*, 41). Moreover, R. C. Sproul observes: "The term ['total depravity'] is misleading because it suggests a moral condition of *utter* depravity. *Utter depravity* means a person is as wicked as he can possibly be. *Utter* suggests both total and complete corruption, lacking even in civil virtue" (*What Is Reformed Theology?*), 117. For an explanation of *civil virtue* see footnote 16 below.

[9] Selph, *Southern Baptists and the Doctrine of Election*, 82–83.

In John 3:19–20 Jesus says:

> And this is the judgment: the light has come
> into the world, and people loved the darkness
> rather than the light because their works were
> evil. For everyone who does wicked things
> hates the light and does not come to the light,
> lest his works should be exposed.

Unregenerate man *cannot* come to Christ because he
will not come to Christ. Left to himself unregenerate
man will inexorably choose darkness over the light
every time.[10] *Why* would he ever come to Christ,
since he has no interest in Christ or the things of God
(Rom. 3:11; 1 Cor. 2:14; 2 Cor. 4:3–4, etc.)? *How*
could he come to Christ, since he has not the ability
to choose Christ of his own initiative? Apart from
the intervening, sovereign grace of God, he *cannot*
choose Christ (John 6:44, 65; Rom. 8:7–8; 1 Cor.
2:14; 2 Cor. 4:3–4, etc.), because he remains in bondage to sin, enslaved to his own iniquities. The sinner
can no more free himself from his own desperate
condition of bondage than can a slave free himself
from his own plight and earthly master.[11] Jesus

[10] Ascol notes: "While it is true that the gospel enables us to say, 'whosoever will,' it is also true that sin forces us to admit that the problem is that
'whosoever' won't! At least, left to himself and his own power of choice he
won't" (*Traditional Theology & the SBC*, 71). Likewise, Selph affirms:
"Man's nature governs his will. He will choose to follow his nature's dic-
tates every time" (*Southern Baptists and the Doctrine of Election*, 88).

[11] John Newton, author of the beloved hymn *Amazing Grace*, made the
following assertion about man's inability to choose Christ apart from sover-

taught this truth in the very next verse (John 3:21): "But whoever does what is true comes to the light, so that it may be clearly seen that his works have been carried out in God." That is to say, in or through union with God, and thus, by His enabling, sovereign grace.

Sovereign Grace

In John 6:35 Jesus says: "I am the bread of life; whoever comes to me shall not hunger, and whoever believes in me shall never thirst." Clearly "comes to" parallels "believes in." The two phrases are synonymous; they mean the same thing. In John 6:37 Jesus says: "All that the Father gives me will come to me, and whoever comes to me I will never cast out." Tom Schreiner remarks:

> This text specifically teaches that only some will come to Jesus, namely, those who have been given by the Father to the Son. In other words, the Father has not given all to the Son; he has selected only some, and it is they who

eign grace: "They who believe there is any power in man by nature, whereby he can turn to God, may contend for a conditional election upon the foresight of faith and obedience; but while others dispute, let you and me admire; for we know that the Lord foresaw us (as we were) in the state *utterly incapable either of believing or obeying*, unless he was pleased to work in us to will and to do according to his own good pleasure" (emphasis added). John Newton, *The Works of the Rev. John Newton* (Edinburgh: Thomas Nelson, 1849), 55.

will come to the Son and believe in him.[12]

This is affirmed by John 6:44 where Jesus explains the reason for unbelief: "No one can come to me unless the Father who sent me draws him. And I will raise him up on the last day." Notice here the necessary condition Jesus points to for acquiring saving faith is the divine drawing of the Father. Again, Schreiner comments: "The word *draw* (*helkuo*), which is used in John 12:32, is also used in John 6:37. The point of John 6:44 is that the Father does not draw all people, only some."[13] Indeed, we know it is only *some* who are drawn and not everyone, because not every individual will be raised up on the last day. Those who are drawn by the Father, Jesus tells us, *will be* raised up on the last day. Then, in John 6:65 Jesus again declares: "This is why I told you that no one can come to me unless it is granted him by the Father." I know of no better commentary on these verses than that of R. C. Sproul:

> The first element of this teaching is a *universal negative*. The words "No one" are all-

---

[12] Thomas R. Schreiner, "Effectual Call and Grace" in *Still Sovereign: Contemporary Perspectives on Election, Foreknowledge, & Grace* (Grand Rapids, MI: Baker Books, 2000), 241.

[13] Ibid. D. A. Carson avers: "The combination of v. 37a and v. 44 prove that this 'drawing' activity of the Father cannot be reduced to what theologians sometimes call 'prevenient grace' dispensed to every individual, for this 'drawing' is selective, or else the negative note in v. 44 is meaningless." D. A. Carson, *The Gospel According to John* (Grand Rapids, MI: Eerdmans, 1991), 293.

inclusive. They allow for no exception apart from the exceptions Jesus adds. The next word is crucial. It is the word *can*. This has to do with ability, not permission. Who has not been corrected by a schoolteacher for confusing the words *can* and *may*? I used to have a teacher who never missed an opportunity to drill this point home. If I raised my hand and said, "Can I sharpen my pencil?" the response was always the same. She would smile and say, "I am sure that you can. You also *may* sharpen your pencil." The word *can* refers to ability; the word *may* refers to permission. In this passage Jesus is not saying, "No one is allowed to come to me. . . ." He is saying, "No one is *able* to come to me. . . ." The next word in the passage is also vital. "Unless" refers to what we call a *necessary condition*. A necessary condition refers to something that must happen before something else can happen. The meaning of Jesus' words is clear. No human being can possibly come to Christ unless something happens that makes it possible for him to come. That necessary condition Jesus declares is that "it has been granted to him by the Father." Jesus is saying here that the ability to come to him is a gift from God. Man does not have the ability in and of himself to come to Christ. God must do something first. The passage teaches at least this much: It is not within fallen man's natural ability to come to Christ on his own without some kind of divine assistance.[14]

The Apostle Paul taught the very same truth. Indeed, Romans 9 is where we find Paul's clearest teaching on *unconditional election*.[15] But leading up to Romans 9, Paul had already established the doctrine of *total depravity* in the preceding chapters. Andy Davis traces this out for us:

> One of the flaws of . . . any basically Arminian view of election is that it finds intrinsic good in sinners prior to God's sovereign working in them.[16] And it does so despite the fact that scripture makes such universally dark statements about sinners prior to regeneration. Romans 3:10–12, "There is none righteous, not even one; there is no one who understands, no one who seeks God. All have

[14] Sproul, *Chosen By God*, 67–68.

[15] We will deal with Romans 9 in chapters 7 and 8.

[16] The Reformers recognized fallen man's ability to do "good" deeds. They referred to this as *civil virtue*. According to Sproul: "*Civil virtue* refers to deeds that conform outwardly to the law of God. Fallen sinners can refrain from stealing and perform acts of charity, but these deeds are not deemed good in an ultimate sense. When God evaluates the actions of people, he considers not only the outward deeds in and of themselves, but also the motives behind these acts. The supreme motive required of everything we do is the love of God. A deed that outwardly conforms to God's law but proceeds from a heart alienated from God is not deemed by God a good deed. The whole action, including the inclinations of the doer's heart, is brought under the scrutiny of God and found wanting" (*What Is Reformed Theology?*, 120).

turned away, they have together become worthless. There is no one who does good, not even one." Romans 4:5 says God justifies "the wicked." Romans 5:6 says we were "powerless," Romans 5:10 says we were "enemies," Romans 6:17 says we were "slaves to sin," and Romans 7:9 says that when God's commands came we died. Romans 8:7 says the mind of the flesh (*i.e.*, the unregenerate mind) is hostile to God, and it does not submit to God's law, indeed it *cannot*. Romans 8:8 says those who are "in the flesh cannot please God." This is the natural state of the human being.[17]

A Stumbling Block

The doctrine of total depravity is a stumbling block for many people.[18] By nature we stubbornly resist

[17] Andy M. Davis, "Unconditional Election: A Biblical and God-Glorifying Doctrine" in *Whosoever He Wills: A Surprising Display of Sovereign Mercy*, eds. Matthew Barrett and Tomas J. Nettles (Cape Coral, FL: Founders Ministries, 2012), 70.

[18] John Gerstner remarks: "The thing that depresses me the most about the objection to unconditional election is that it acts as a red herring. *What people really are objecting to is total depravity.* It is as if a person comes to a physician complaining of a pain in his shoulder only to be told that there's nothing wrong with his shoulder. He is suffering from gallbladder trouble, but the symptom appears in the shoulder. Most people are like this fictional patient in a spiritual sense. Those who object to [predestination] are actually suffering from a lack of conviction of their depravity. Only if you are convinced that you are not just sick, but dead, will you know that there is only one person who can make you alive—the giver of life himself—and therefore be utterly persuaded of the decree of unconditional election" (emphasis added). John R. Gerstner, *Atonement*, ed. Gabriel N. E. Fluhrer (Phillipsburg, NJ: P&R Publishing, 2010), 54.

this doctrine. We are convinced that, even in our fallen state, there is still some intrinsic good in us—at least enough good to turn to Christ on our own. We twist Paul's words in Romans 3:10–12 to mean something other than what they plainly say: "None is righteous, no, not one; no one understands; no one seeks for God. All have turned aside; together they have become worthless; no one does good, not even one."[19] But once we understand what the Bible teaches about human depravity and accept its unambiguous teaching about our fallen nature, we will be begging for sovereign grace—and rejoicing over Romans 9![20]

Non-Calvinist Proof Texts

From time to time, we will end the chapter by examining a few proof texts typically cited by non-Calvinists to support their point of view. In this case, it is the belief that unregenerate man has libertarian

---

[19] John Piper is surely right when he states: "It is a myth that man in his natural state is genuinely seeking God. Men do seek God. But they do not seek him for who he is. They seek him in a pinch as one who might preserve them from death or enhance their worldly enjoyments. Apart from conversion, no one comes to the light of God." John Piper, *Five Points: Towards a Deeper Experience of God's Grace*, (Ross-shire, UK: Christian Focus, 2013), 19.

[20] Indeed, once a person begins to understand the biblical doctrine of total depravity, they will soon find themselves embracing the other four points of Calvinism as well. As Sproul insists: "The moral inability of fallen man is the core of the doctrine of total depravity . . . If one embraces this aspect of the T in TULIP, the rest of the acrostic follows by a resistless logic. One cannot embrace the T and reject any of the other four letters with any degree of consistency" (*What Is Reformed Theology?*, 128).

freedom despite the totality of the biblical teaching about our fallen state, and despite the poignant reality of Paul's words in Romans. It is often assumed, or taken for granted, that God provides "prevenient grace" to sinners, rendering all people morally neutral whereby they can freely choose or reject the gospel invitation of their own "free will." But is this truly the biblical teaching, or is it an assumption foisted upon the text of Scripture? The first text we will consider is Acts 16:31.

> And they said, "Believe in the Lord Jesus, and you will be saved, you and your household."

This verse does not prove that man has libertarian freedom. Rather, it tells us *what* is demanded of sinners (belief); it does not tell us *how* belief occurs (by sovereign grace). Verses such as Acts 16:31 must be interpreted in view of the totality of Scripture (*tota Scriptura*). Indeed, divine sovereignty and human responsibility, like two parallel tracks, run throughout the Bible.[21] Sometimes we even find both truths taught in a single verse or passage (Matt. 11:27–30; Luke 22:22; Acts 2:23, etc.). John 1:12–13 is a perfect example of this, and we will cite it as the next proof text to be considered.

> But to all who did receive him, who believed

---

[21] We will discuss this matter in more detail in chapter 8.

in his name, he gave the right to become children of God, who were born, not of blood nor of the will of the flesh nor of the will of man, but of God.

Note that v. 12 emphasizes man's responsibility to believe while v. 13 emphasizes God's sovereignty in salvation. Verse 12 does not *prove* that man has libertarian freedom. Rather, v. 12 tells us the *what* (believers in Jesus have an adopted status as the children of God) and v. 13 gives us the *how* (by sovereign grace).[22] Tom Ascol explains:

> Verse 12 teaches that those who receive Christ were authorized to become children of God—adopted into his family. Verse 13 explains how that happened by speaking of the act of birth. . . . Those who are adopted into God's family entered into that privileged status because they believed. They believed because they had been born (again) wholly and exclusively by the work of God. John specifically and plainly denies that their spiritual birth came through their genealogy ("not of blood") or through the exercise of their will ("the will of the flesh") or through the imposition of an-

[22] Andreas Kostenberger affirms: "In John 1:12, the focus is on 'becoming' God's children, indicating change of status. . . . [In John 1:13] spiritual birth is not the result of human initiative ... but of a supernatural origin." Andreas J. Kostenbeger, *John* in Baker Exegetical Commentary on the New Testament (Grand Rapids, MI: Baker Academic, 2004), 39.

other's will ("nor of the will of man"). Rather, those who are children of God enter into that status *because they have been monergistically born . . . of God*. So in terms of the application of salvation, this passage teaches that it flows like this: *new birth—faith—adoption*.[23] It is impossible to reconcile synergistic regeneration with these verses (emphasis added).[24]

Unfortunately for non-Calvinists, John 1:12–13 only serves to refute their view of (libertarian) free will. This passage visibly teaches that man's response to the free call of the gospel (v. 12) occurs as a result of God's will, not man's (v. 13; see also Rom. 9:16; 1 Pet. 1:3, 23; Jas. 1:18, etc.).

---

[23] We will discuss more fully the order of salvation in chapter 6.

[24] Ascol, *Traditional Theology & the SBC*, 55. See pp. 25–27 for an explanation of *monergism* and *synergism*.

4

For Whom Did Christ Die?

Two Streams of Thought

The atoning death of Christ is a deeply profound and mysterious subject. Some Calvinists believe the atonement is *sufficient* for all, but *efficient* only for the elect.[1] Others believe the atonement was *suffi-*

---

[1] George observes: "Since the Middle Ages, many theologians, including Thomas Aquinas and John Calvin, have made this distinction: Jesus' death is *sufficient* to save all, but it is *efficient* to save only those who repent and believe the gospel" (*Amazing Grace*, 92). Among those who hold this position is D. A. Carson, who writes: "Both Arminians and Calvinists should rightly affirm that Christ died for all, in the sense that Christ's death was sufficient for all and that Scripture portrays God as inviting, commanding, and desiring the salvation of all. . . . Further, all Christians ought also to confess that, in a slightly different sense, Christ Jesus, in the intent of God, died effectively for the elect alone, *in line with the way the Bible speaks of God's special selecting love for the elect* . . ." D. A. Carson, *The Difficult Doctrine of the Love of God* (Wheaton, IL: Crossway, 2000), 77. Likewise, John Piper avers: "We do not deny that Christ died to save all *in some sense*. Paul says in 1 Timothy 4:10 that in Christ God is 'the Savior of all people, especially of those who believe.' What we deny is that the death of Christ is for all men in the *same* sense. God sent Christ to save *all* in some sense. And he sent Christ to save those who believe in *a more particular sense*. God's intention is different for each. That is a natural way to read 1 Timothy 4:10"

cient only for the elect.[2] Tom Nettles observes:

> Historically, two streams of thought emerge from the writings of those who have defended limited atonement. We must not confuse either with those who purposefully rejected limited atonement. One stream, represented by such Baptists as [Andrew] Fuller in England and [James] Boyce in the United States, *affirms both the sufficiency of the atonement in its nature to save all men and the limitation of the atonement to the elect only in its intent.* This probably represents a majority view among Calvinists. The second stream, represented by Abraham Booth in England and John L. Dagg in the United States, *affirms that it is the nature of the atonement to save all for whom it is sufficient, and therefore its limitation in intent is necessarily a limitation of its sufficiency* (emphasis added).[3]

(*Five Points*, 40–41).

[2] On the surface at least, some Scripture passages do seem to teach that Christ died for the whole world *in some sense* (John 3:16; 1 Timothy 4:10; 2 Timothy 2:3–6; 1 John 2:2, etc.). The question is, do these texts refer to every human being who has ever lived, or do they refer to every people group without distinction? For more on this see the discussion below under the heading "Non-Calvinist Proof Texts."

[3] Nettles, *By His Grace and for His Glory*, 340. Incidentally, Nettles is among those who believe the atonement was sufficient only for the elect. He contends that those who take the opposing position do so "fearing that the sinful creature might charge God with injustice unless a sufficient atonement has been made for *all* men" (Ibid., 343). Nettles further states: "The Apostle Paul never discusses the atonement in terms of rendering men inexcusable. What makes a man inexcusable is his rejection of the knowledge and law of

Resolving the Tension

The pertinent question is this: How do we square the "universal texts" (John 3:16, etc.) with others that clearly point to a *limited* (or *definite*) *atonement*— that Christ accomplished redemption only for a particular group of people?

One of the primary reasons I am a Calvinist is because I am convinced that the Calvinist hermeneutic (*i.e.*, approach to interpreting Scripture) is far better at harmonizing Scripture than the non-Calvinist approach.[4] In this case, what must be harmonized is the apparent tension between *general* atonement (Christ died for everyone) and *definite* atonement (Christ died for a definite number of people, that is, for the elect only). On this matter, Lee Gatiss writes:

> The question of the extent or intent of the atonement arises directly out of serious Bible

God in nature, on the heart, and in special revelation (Romans 1:18–20; 3:19–20). Atonement is not designed to render one inexcusable; atonement is designed to save justly some of those who already stand inexcusable and under condemnation. God was certainly under no obligation to provide atonement for even one man, much less all men. The absolute particularity of the atonement needs no more apology than does effectual call or unconditional election. If the theologian must become enamored with demonstrating how God's activity releases him from any likelihood of impugnation, both election and calling would have to be defended in the same way" (Ibid., 344).

[4] Sproul asserts: "Reformed theology is systematic. The science of systematic theology is so called because it attempts to understand doctrine in a coherent and unified manner. It is not the goal of systematic theology to impose on the Bible a system derived from a particular philosophy. Rather, its goal is to discern the interrelatedness of the teachings of Scripture itself" (*What Is Reformed Theology?*, 23).

study when scripture itself is used to interpret scripture. Those who hold to limited atonement therefore believe that it makes more sense of the Bible's witness as a whole. They would suggest that the supposedly "straightforward" yet atomistic reading of universal texts creates more problems *biblically* than it solves. If we are to reject the doctrine of definite atonement *simply* because 1 John 2:2 says Jesus was the propitiation "not for our sins only, but for the sins of the whole world," then must we not also reject the Protestant doctrine of justification *simply* because James 2:24 says "a person is justified by works and not by faith alone"? The desire for a tidy system of theology with neat resolutions to every difficulty is understandable, even if it may not be entirely achievable. On the other hand, it would be shallow simply to lay seemingly contradictory statements from the Bible side by side and not attempt to understand how they cohere. It would be especially irresponsible to do this if the Bible itself gives us clues as to how they might be harmonized. To take refuge in paradox or "mystery" too quickly and easily is to miss out on the fullness of the word, which God has given us for our delight and obedience. We are meant to chew on these things, not wolf them down whole without further thought.[5]

Only Three Options Available

The question we must ask is this: *For whom did Christ die? More specifically, did Jesus die to pay for the sins of every single human being?* If true, then we are confronted with two inescapable conclusions: either (1) *universalism* (the view that everyone will ultimately be restored to a right relationship with God and will forever enjoy communion with Him) is the biblical teaching, or (2) *God is unjust* for condemning people to everlasting punishment whose sins have already been atoned for on the cross. The problem is that no consistent Bible-believing Christian could ever affirm *either* of these views as a viable interpretation of Scripture. Consequently, *everyone* limits the atonement in some way or other (which is one reason many Calvinists prefer the terms *definite atonement* or *particular redemption*).[6] Regarding this, Horton writes:

[5] Lee Gatiss, *For Us and For Our Salvation: 'Limited Atonement' in the Bible, Doctrine, History, and Ministry* (London, UK: The Latimer Trust, 2012), 20–21.

[6] As Gatiss recognizes: "So both Calvinists and Arminians believe in 'limited atonement' in some sense! The question is, what is it that imposes the limitation? Is it God in his wise design, or is it humanity in its free choice?" (Ibid., 16). Likewise, Ascol maintains: "Everyone 'limits' or particularizes the atonement in some way, unless universalism is affirmed. Either the atoning work of Jesus is limited in its scope—that is, intended only for particular people, or it is limited in its efficacy—that is, not able to save the very people for whom it was intended" (*Traditional Theology & the SBC*, 43).

As the seventeenth–century Puritan John Owen observed, every position that recognizes that some will finally be lost places a limit on the atonement at some point—either it is limited in its extent or in its effect. Owen summarizes the options: Christ died for (1) all of the sins of all people; (2) some of the sins of all people, or (3) all of the sins of some people. If unbelief is a sin and some people are finally condemned, there is at least one sin for which Christ did not make adequate satisfaction.[7]

Option one leads to *universalism* (everyone will be saved). Option two results in *no one* being saved. That leaves option three, which is the Calvinist position. The non-Calvinist might object, insisting that option one is the biblical teaching on the atonement. The argument often goes something like this: "Christ's death atones for all of the sins of all people. Of course, not everyone will be saved because not everyone believes in Jesus for salvation. Consequently, they are eternally lost due to their own unbelief." But this begs the question: Is *unbelief* a sin? Indeed it is. So if Christ died for all of the sins of all people— including their unbelief—then what? James Boice and Philip Ryken provide the only logical conclusion:

---

[7] Horton, *For Calvinism*, 92. John Owen, "The Death of Death in the Death of Christ" in *Works of John Owen* (Edinburg: Banner of Truth Trust, 1966), 10:233.

Is unbelief a morally neutral choice, merely deciding to accept or not accept salvation? Or is it a sin? It is a sin, of course. In fact, it is the most damnable of all sins, for it is the equivalent of trampling the very blood of the Son of God underfoot. But this means—if Jesus died for all the sins of all men, including the sin of unbelief—that all are saved, and we are back to universalism.[8]

It Is Finished!

Definite atonement means that God's purpose in election was actually accomplished with the death of Christ. The author of Hebrews makes this abundantly clear when he wrote that the death of Jesus *obtained eternal redemption* (Heb. 9:12). God did not send His Son into the world to make redemption merely *possible* for everyone, but rather, to make salvation *certain* for His own. Christ's death atoned for the sins of a *definite* number, a *particular* people, the "elect" of God (Rom. 8:34). The Bible teaches that Christ died for *His sheep* (John 10:11, 15, 17:6, 9, 19); for *His friends* (John 15:13); to save *His people* (Matt. 1:21); to gather *God's children* (John 11:50–52); as a ransom for *many* (Isa. 53:12; Matt. 26:28; Mark 10:45; Heb. 9:28; Rev. 5:9); and for *the Church* (Acts 20:28; Eph. 5:25–27).[9]

[8] Boice and Ryken, *The Doctrines of Grace*, 123–124.
[9] See Piper, *Five Points*, 46–50.

In a sermon titled "Particular Redemption," the legendary Baptist preacher, Charles H. Spurgeon, stated the following:

> We hold that Christ, when He died, had an objective in view and that objective will most assuredly and beyond a doubt, be accomplished! . . . We do not believe that Christ made any effectual Atonement for those who are forever damned! We dare not think that the blood of Christ was ever shed with the intention of saving those whom God foreknew would be saved—and some of whom were even in Hell when Christ, according to some men's account, died to save them! . . . Now, beloved, when you hear any one laughing or jeering at a limited atonement, you may tell him this. General atonement is like a great wide bridge with only half an arch; it does not go across the stream: it only professes to go half way; it does not secure the salvation of anybody. Now, I had rather put my foot upon a bridge as narrow as Hungerford, which went all the way across, than a bridge that was as wide as the world, if it did not go all the way across the stream.[10]

Christ did not die to make redemption merely *possible* for all humanity. Rather, Christ died to

[10] Sermon 181, cited in Ascol, *Traditional Theology & the SBC*, 44–45.

make salvation *certain* for His own people. It is finished (John 19:30); our salvation is secured!

Non-Calvinist Proof Texts

Before we conclude the chapter, let us examine a couple of proof texts often cited by non-Calvinists to "prove" that Christ died for every single person without exception. The first proof text we'll consider is Romans 5:18.

> Therefore, as one trespass led to condemnation for all men, so one act of righteousness leads to justification and life for all men.

Before we deal with this verse, we would do well to consider the following comments by Lee Gatiss:

> Both "world" . . . and "all" . . . should not immediately be assumed to mean "everyone without exception," since they are used in scripture in a variety of ways. . . . To show that we must be careful with this, consider various Old and New Testament examples. In Genesis 6:13, 17 God determines to destroy "all flesh". . . . The context (the whole story!) shows, however, that this does not include Noah, his extended family, and the large number of animals he is told to save. Luke 2:1 ("all the world should be registered") does not envisage the entire population of the

planet taking part in a Roman census. Matthew 3:5–6 ("all Judea") does not mean to suggest that every single man, woman, and child in Judea without exception went out and was baptised by John, especially since Luke 7:30 explicitly says that the Pharisees and lawyers were *not* baptised by him. Acts 2:17 ("I will pour out my Spirit on all flesh") does not mean that everyone in the world was given the Holy Spirit at the first Pentecost. . . . So it cannot simply mean "all without exception" . . . Context must always be taken into account, to establish the implied sphere of reference.[11]

With these helpful thoughts in mind, we note that in Romans 5:18 Paul is not teaching that Christ died for all men without *exception*; rather, Christ died for all men without *distinction* (Jew or Gentile). Read in isolation from the rest of Scripture this verse could plausibly suggest *universalism* (that everyone will be saved). So we need to look at this verse in context. Romans 5:17–19 says:

For if, because of one man's trespass, death reigned through that one man, much more will those who receive the abundance of grace and the free gift of righteousness reign in life through the one man Jesus Christ. Therefore,

---

[11] Gatiss, *For Us and For Our Salvation*, 42–44.

as one trespass led to condemnation for all men, so one act of righteousness leads to justification and life for all men. For as by the one man's disobedience the many were made sinners, so by the one man's obedience the many will be made righteous.

Verse 17 makes it clear that the "all men" of v. 18 are those who "receive the abundance of grace and the free gift of righteousness" (that is, *believers* in Christ). Therefore, as we previously stated, v. 18 does not refer to all men without *exception*, but rather, to all men without *distinction*. And v. 19 means that believers are considered righteous in the sense of legal standing.

The same truth applies to 2 Corinthians 5:14–15, 18–19:

For the love of Christ controls us, because we have concluded this: that one has died for all, therefore all have died; and he died for all, that those who live might no longer live for themselves but for him who for their sake died and was raised. . . . All this is from God, who through Christ reconciled us to himself and gave us the ministry of reconciliation; that is, in Christ God was reconciling the world to himself, not counting their trespasses against them, and entrusting to us the message of reconciliation.

Again, the "alls" refer to all humanity without *distinction* (Jew or Gentile) who are in Christ by faith. In v. 14 the ones for whom Christ died are the same as the "all (who have) died" with Him (Gal. 2:20; Rom. 6:1–14).

Finally, let us consider Matthew 23:37:

> O Jerusalem, Jerusalem, the city that kills the prophets and stones those who are sent to it! How often would I have gathered your children together as a hen gathers her brood under her wings, and you were not willing!

This verse fails to prove that God desires for every single human being to be saved as non-Calvinists insist. Rather, this verse affirms Jesus' compassion for the lost, His sorrow over Israel's rejection of Him as their Messiah, and that He takes no pleasure in the death of the wicked (Ezek. 18:23; 33:11). Again, Matthew 23:37 and other such verses (1 Tim. 2:4; 2 Pet. 3:9, etc.) must be interpreted in view of the whole of Scripture with a view toward consistency of message. The Bible affirms both God's universal love for the world *and* God's special love for the elect (see chapter 7).[12] God wills that no one should perish *and*

---

[12] Historically, Reformed theology has affirmed God's love for all of humanity. Regarding John 3:16, John Calvin himself remarked: "As the whole matter of our salvation must not be sought anywhere else than in Christ, so we must see whence Christ came to us, and why he was offered to be our Savior. Both points are distinctly stated to us: namely, that faith in Christ brings life to all, and that Christ brought life, because the Heavenly

to elect unconditionally some for salvation. Let us admit that God's will is a mystery that we will never fully comprehend, much less be able to explain to our complete satisfaction. Even the renowned Arminian scholar, I. H. Marshall, admits: "We must distinguish between what God would like to see happen and what he actually does will to happen, and both of these things can be spoken of as God's will."[13]

God wills that no one should perish *and* to elect unconditionally some for salvation. And we must affirm what the Bible affirms! We conclude with these thought provoking words by Piper:

> My aim is to let Scripture stand—to let it teach what it will and not to tell it what it cannot say. Sometimes I hear people say that we who adhere to unconditional election are controlled more by the demands of logic than by the demands of Scripture. . . . On the contrary, it seems to me that more often philosophical assumptions cause the *rejection* of election. For example, the statement, 'God cannot choose individuals unconditionally

Father loves the human race, and wished that they should not perish." John Calvin, *Commentary on a Harmony of the Evangelists, Matthew, Mark, and Luke*, Vol. 3, trans. William Pringle (Grand Rapids, MI: Baker, Reprinted Edition, 2005), 123.

[13] I. H. Marshall, "Universal Grace and Atonement in the Pastoral Epistles" in *A Case for Arminianism* (Grand Rapids, MI: Zondervan Publishing House, 1989) 56.

and yet have compassion on all men,' is based on a certain kind of philosophical assumption, not on Scripture. Scripture leads us precisely to this paradoxical position. I am willing to let the paradox stand even if I can't explain it. It seems to me that those who teach against unconditional election are often controlled by non-biblical logic. . . . They deny that the Bible teaches unconditional election because it teaches things they can't fit together with election. This, however, is not the method I follow. I do not deny that Jesus wept over Jerusalem. I do not deny that he felt genuine compassion for perishing people. I do not deny that God loves the world of lost men—elect and non-elect. On the contrary, all I want to do is try to give an account for how both of these biblical teachings can be so—the plain teaching of the Bible on election *and* the plain teaching that God has sincere compassion for the non-elect which he expresses in various ways in the Bible. I do not allow some alien logic to force me to choose between these two teachings of Scripture.[14]

[14] John Piper, *The Pleasures of God: Meditations on God's Delight in Being God* (Colorado Springs, CO: Multnomah Books, 2000), 146–147.

5

Does God Save the Unwilling?

According to Norman Geisler: "There is no biblical support for irresistible grace on the unwilling. All can, and some do, resist God's grace (Matt. 23:37; cf. 2 Pet. 3:9)."[1] To the contrary, there is a wealth of biblical support for irresistible grace on the unwilling. Not only *can all* but *all do* resist God's grace, yet God's grace overcomes the resistance of *some*. Furthermore, if God's grace did not overcome the resistance of *some*, then *none* would be saved!

Overcoming Grace

A common caricature non-Calvinists frequently make about Calvinism is this: "Only those God has predestined will be saved, and we have no choice in

[1] Norman L. Geisler, *Chosen But Free: A Balanced View of God's Sovereignty and Free Will,* Third Edition (Bloomington, MN: Bethany House Publishers, 2010), 283.

the matter." In other words, God saves us in spite of our desires and against our will. But as we saw in chapter 3, we *do* have a choice. In the work of regeneration God changes the disposition of the unregenerate heart and gives the desire for Christ. As Jonathan Edwards observed: "The first effect of the power of God in the heart in regeneration, is to give the heart a divine taste or sense; to cause it to have a relish of the loveliness and sweetness of the supreme excellency of the divine nature."[2] But here is the point we dare not miss: Once this change in the heart has been wrought, *we choose* to come to Christ *freely* and *willingly*, not by coercion as some maintain.

Because of our sinful, rebellious nature, every human being resists God's grace (John 3:19–20; Rom. 1:21; 3:11, 18, 8:7; 1 Cor. 2:14: 2 Cor. 4:3–4; Rom. 5:10; Col. 1:21, etc.). However, God graciously *overcomes* the sinner's natural inclination to resist His saving grace. This is the doctrine often referred to as *irresistible grace*. It is not that God drags people into His kingdom "kicking and screaming" (as some non-Calvinists allege). Rather, it is that God overcomes our resistance to His grace by taking away "the heart of stone" and giving us "a heart of flesh" (Ezek. 11:19–20, 36:26–27; Deut. 30:6; Jer. 32:39). Sproul provides a helpful explanation of

[2] Jonathan Edwards, *Treatise on Grace*, ed. Paul Helm (Cambridge: James Clarke and Co., 1971), 48–49.

this term when he writes:

> Irresistible grace is not irresistible in the sense
> that sinners are incapable of resisting it.
> Though the sinner is spiritually dead, he re-
> mains biologically alive and kicking. As Scrip-
> ture suggests, the sinner always resists the Ho-
> ly Spirit. We are so opposed to the grace of
> God that we do everything in our power to
> resist it. *Irresistible grace* means that the sin-
> ner's resistance to the grace of regeneration
> cannot thwart the Spirit's purpose. The grace
> of regeneration is irresistible in the sense that
> it is invincible.[3]

Because the term "irresistible" is subject to being
misunderstood, many Calvinists prefer to use other
terms instead. Consequently, I agree with George
who writes:

> I like the term *overcoming grace* because it
> conveys the truth witnessed to by so many
> Christians: despite their stubbornness and re-
> bellion, they say, God did not give up on
> them. Like a persistent lover, he kept on woo-
> ing until, at last, his persistence won the day.
> His love and mercy overcame their rebellious
> resistance.[4]

---

[3] Sproul, *What Is Reformed Theology?*, 189.
[4] George, *Amazing Grace*, 86. I also love the way Jim Orrick puts it:
"When a person repents of sin and believes in Christ, it is evidence that God

57

Effectual Calling

Another term for irresistible grace is *effectual calling*. Those whom God has elected unto salvation He effectively calls and regenerates. Or, as Orrick puts it: "God's call always produces the desired effect in the sinner, and so we say it is an effectual call."[5] Likewise, Sproul affirms: "Effectual calling is effectual because in it and by it God effects exactly what he intends in the operation: the quickening of spiritually dead souls to spiritual life. *Calling* refers to the Holy Spirit's inward or secret operation on the soul."[6] Scripture teaches that there is also a *general calling* that is universal. The general call goes out to everyone who hears the preaching of the gospel (Matt. 11:28–30; Rev. 22:17, etc.). But the effectual call only comes to God's elect.

Of course, non-Calvinists claim there isn't a shred of evidence in Scripture for an effectual call. To the contrary, there is plenty of evidence. Space will not allow us to examine but a few of these passages, but these will suffice. The first text we will consider is 1 Corinthians 1:22–24:

> For Jews demand signs and Greeks seek wisdom, but we preach Christ crucified, a stum-

---

has worked in the sinner so that he has stopped resisting God. He has been *sweetly compelled* by God's irresistible grace" (*Mere Calvinism*, 136 [emphasis mine]).

[5] Ibid.

[6] Sproul, *What Is Reformed Theology*, 190.

bling block to Jews and folly to Gentiles, but
to those who are called, both Jews and
Greeks, Christ the power of God and the wisdom of God.

We actually see both the general and the effectual
call in this passage. The general call goes out to everyone who hears the preaching of the gospel. Paul
says "we preach Christ crucified" to both Jews and
Gentiles. *Some* Jews stumbled over it and *some* Gentiles considered it folly, but *all* heard the message and
thus received the *general* call. However, *some* within
this larger group (of Jews and Gentiles) received
both the general and the effectual call. Note carefully
what Paul says in verse 24: "but to those who are
called, both Jews and Gentiles, Christ the power of
God and the wisdom of God." What call is this? It is
the *effectual call!* Clearly there is a distinction being
made here. Matthew Barrett comments:

This specific group ("the called ones") is in
contrast to the larger group of Jews and
Greeks whom Paul says received the message
of Christ crucified and saw it as a stumbling
block (Jews) and as folly (Gentiles). On the
other hand, to the "called ones" Christ is the
power and wisdom of God. Such a contrast
precludes any idea that Paul is only referring

to a general gospel call.[7]

I want to say, "Case closed!" But let us look at another important passage that teaches there is an effectual call.

Divine Foreknowledge and Effectual Calling

In Romans 8:28–30 Paul writes:

> And we know that for those who love God all things work together for good, for those who are called according to his purpose. For those whom he foreknew he also predestined to be conformed to the image of his Son, in order that he might be the firstborn among many brothers. And those whom he predestined he also called, and those whom he called he also justified, and those whom he justified he also glorified.

[7] Matthew M. Barrett, "A Scriptural Affirmation of Monergism" in *Whosoever He Wills: A Surprising Display of Sovereign Mercy*, eds. Matthew Barrett and Thomas J. Nettles (Cape Coral, FL: Founders Ministries, 2012), 131. David Steele, Curtis Thomas and Lance Quinn contend: "The general call of the gospel can be, and often is rejected, but the special call of the Spirit cannot be rejected; it always results in the conversion of those to whom it is made." David N. Steele, Curtis C. Thomas and S. Lance Quinn, *The Five Points of Calvinism: Defined, Defended, and Documented*, Updated and Expanded (Phillipsburg, NJ: P&R Publishing, 2004), 61. Sproul concurs: "We find God's external call in the preaching of the gospel. When the gospel is preached, everyone who hears it is summoned to Christ. But not everyone responds positively. Not everyone who hears the outward call of the gospel becomes a believer. Sometimes the gospel falls on deaf ears" (*Chosen By God*, 131).

Commenting on this passage, Geisler makes this assertion:

> This and other Scriptures reveal that election is related to foreknowledge. Romans 8:29 . . . says: "For those whom he foreknew he also predestined." And 1 Peter proclaims that the elect "have been chosen *according to the foreknowledge of God* the Father." This affirms that God is the unconditional source of the election and that election is done with full foreknowledge of all things. Election is not *based on* or dependent on foreknowledge. Rather, election is *in accord with it*.[8]

Really? Pay close attention to what Paul actually says here. Contra Geisler, Paul does not say: "For those whom he foreknew *would believe upon His Son* he predestined . . ."[9] If that is what Paul meant

---

[8] Geisler, *Chosen But Free*, 67.

[9] Geisler makes the same argument regarding Ephesians 1:4 which says: "he chose us in him before the foundation of the world . . ." Geisler remarks: "What then is the connection between God knowing we will believe and God choosing (electing) us for salvation (Eph. 1:4)? It is simply this: God knowingly decided and decidedly knew from all eternity who would believe and be saved and who would not. And, 'in accordance with' this foreknowledge, He chose to save those who would believe" (Ibid., 150). Frank Page agrees: "The Bible teaches that God elected a plan of salvation (Ephesians 1–2). He predestined that all who receive Jesus Christ would be part of His elect family. He knew in advance exactly who would make that decision and who would not. . . . It was His plan to predestine the way of redemption. In other words, He did indeed predestine the *how* of redemption, not the *who*. To believe otherwise would be to deny God's gift of individual conscience, decision making power, and free will." Frank S. Page, *Trouble with the Tulip: A Closer Examination of the Five Points of Calvin-*

then he passed up a golden opportunity to say so. No, Paul says: "For those whom he foreknew he also predestined . . ." That is to say, God foreknew *people*, not facts about them or events.[10] The Greek word for *foreknew* in verse 29a emphasizes God's special choice.[11] It pertains to God's intimate knowledge of His elect from eternity past. Even the Arminian scholar, I. Howard Marshall, admits this: "It is generally agreed that the 'knowing' in this verb must be understood in the Hebraic sense of fixing one's loving regard upon a person."[12] Regarding Romans 8:29a, Robert Peterson notes: "God planned to set his love upon them, to enter into a saving per-

ism, Second Edition (Canton, GA: Riverstone Group, 2006), 44-45. This is the epitome of eisegesis (reading one's own ideas into the text)! Ascol is surely right when he states: "The object of 'chose' (*exelexato*) in verse 4 is 'us'—people, believers—not a plan. ... God is the subject of Paul's sentence. 'Chose' is the verb. 'Us' is the object. My view of inspiration will not allow me to deviate from the plain meaning of this plain statement. The object of election is people, not a plan" (*Traditional Theology & the SBC*, 59).

[10] Davis writes: "The Greek verb translated 'foreknew' ... does not necessarily imply knowledge about something, although it certainly could have that meaning. The real issue in Romans 8:29 is the grammar which makes it obvious that it is people specifically that God foreknows. The direct object of the verb is the relative pronoun οὓς ('those,' meaning 'those people whom . . .'). This brings a deeper sense of how it is that God knows people, and not just things about people" ("Unconditional Election," 64–65).

[11] Commenting on Romans 8:29a Douglas Moo writes: "'Know' probably has the biblical sense of 'enter into relationship with' (see Gen 18:19; Jer 1:5; Amos 3:2, where the same Hebrew word is translated 'chosen,' 'knew,' and 'chosen,' respectively): God chose to initiate a relationship with people 'before the creation of the world' (Eph 1:4; cf. Rom 11:2; Acts 2:23; 1 Pet 1:2, 20) and on that basis 'predestined' them." Douglas J. Moo, *Romans* in The NIV Zondervan Study Bible, ed. D. A. Carson, (Grand Rapids, MI: Zondervan, 2015), 2307.

[12] I. Howard Marshall, *Kept By the Power of God: A Study of Perseverance and Falling Away* (London, UK: Epworth Press, 1969), 93.

sonal relationship with them. If we inquire when this took place, we learn from the teaching of other Scriptures that God did this 'before the foundation of the world' (Eph 1:4) and 'before the ages began' (2 Tim 1:9)."[13]

So how is divine foreknowledge related to an effectual call? The promise given in Romans 8:28 is clearly for believers only. Paul identifies them as "those who are called according to his purpose." God's "purpose" is His purpose of election, which Paul unfolds in Romans 8:29–30: "For those whom he foreknew [chose] he also predestined to be conformed to the image of his Son . . . And those whom he predestined he also called, and those whom he called he also justified, and those whom he justified he also glorified." This *cannot* possibly be referring to the general call. Why not? Because not everyone is justified and glorified! As Peterson observes: "Those foreknown are the same ones who are predestined, called, justified, and glorified. Because it is clear that not everyone will be glorified, it follows that not everyone is foreknown or loved beforehand."[14]

---

[13] Robert A. Peterson, *Election and Free Will: God's Gracious Choice and Our Responsibility* in Explorations of Biblical Theology Series, ed. Robert A. Peterson (Phillipsburg, NJ: P&R Publishing, 2007), 112.

[14] Ibid. Ascol declares: "If there is no distinction between the call of God that results in salvation through the effectual working of the Holy Spirit and the general call of the gospel that goes out every time the gospel is preached, then we are forced to conclude from this 'golden chain of salvation' that everyone who is called by hearing the gospel will be justified and glorified" (*Traditional Theology & the SBC*, 75–76).

Moreover, Article VIII on "Regeneration" of the *Abstract of Principles* affirms the Spirit's effectual calling when it states:

> Regeneration is a change of heart, wrought by the Holy Spirit, who quickeneth the dead in trespasses and sins enlightening their minds spiritually and savingly to understand the Word of God, and renewing their whole nature, so that they love and practice holiness. It is a work of God's free and special grace alone.

The entire article affirms *monergism*,[15] but the word "alone" in the final sentence is especially noteworthy.

The Effectual Calling of God

At the end of chapter 1, we cited a couple of quotes about Calvinism by the famous English Baptist preacher, C. H. Spurgeon. We conclude this chapter with some remarks by the popular Southern Baptist pastor, W. A. Criswell. The following excerpt is taken from a sermon he preached in 1983 on Romans 9:15–16 titled "The Effectual Calling of God":

> *There is a general call, but there is also an effective call.* In the great general call, most of

[15] See pp. 25–27.

them did not respond, most of them did not hear, most of them did not believe, most of them did not come; but always some came, some heard, some were saved— *the effectual calling of God*. I read in Acts 13, verse 48, "When the Gentiles heard this, they were glad, and glorified the Word of the Lord: and as many as were ordained to eternal life believed." I turn the page again, and I read in Thessalonians chapter 2, "Brethren beloved, because God hath from the beginning chosen you to salvation, whereunto He called you by our gospel." *There is an effectual call*. There are those who listen. God opens their hearts. God speaks to them, and they hear their name called, and they respond; *the effectual calling of the elective choosing Spirit of the Lord* (emphasis added).[16]

Don't miss the subtle point being made by Criswell that he sees the doctrine of effectual calling everywhere in Scripture. Thank God for irresistible grace. If not for that, *none* would be saved!

---

[16] Cited in ibid., 77; available at https://www.wacriswell.com/sermons/1983/the-effectual-calling-of-god1/.

6

Does Regeneration Precede Faith?

Calvinists believe that *regeneration precedes faith*. That is, faith is the result of regeneration rather than its cause, as non-Calvinists believe. On the surface, this may seem illogical. But as we will see in this chapter, this doctrine is firmly rooted in Scripture.

According to Reformed theology, the order of salvation is as follows: election, calling, regeneration, conversion (faith/repentance), justification, adoption, sanctification, and glorification. Note that regeneration *precedes* faith. Technically speaking, however, a person is *not* "saved" before they express faith, since according to Ephesians 2:8, faith is a necessary condition for salvation. Admittedly, though, from a human standpoint it is impossible to distinguish between the various components in the order of salvation. As John Piper asserts:

The two acts (new birth and faith) are so closely connected that in experience we cannot distinguish them. God begets us anew and the first glimmer of life in the newborn child is faith. Thus new birth is the effect of irresistible grace, because it is an act of sovereign creation.[1]

The Sovereign Work of the Spirit

Regeneration precedes faith. Nowhere is this more clearly demonstrated than in the Gospel of John. In John 3:1–8 Jesus taught that the new birth is the sovereign work of the Holy Spirit. Nicodemus could not bring about his own spiritual birth any more than he could his own natural birth. In verse 3 Jesus says: "Unless one is born again he cannot see the kingdom of God." Then, in verse 5 he says: "Unless one is born of water and the Spirit, he cannot enter the kingdom of God." *Seeing* and *entering* are metaphors for *believing*. The word *can* has to do with *ability*.

The word *unless* is a necessary condition. Consequently, no one can "see" or "enter" the kingdom of God (believe) unless they first experience the new birth (regeneration) which is wrought by the Holy Spirit. The obvious implication is that regeneration precedes faith. According to Matthew Barrett: "In John 3:3–7 there is not a hint of indication that the

[1] Piper, *Five Points*, 35.

new birth has anything to do with the human will. To the contrary, Jesus is emphasizing, through the image of birth, the passivity and inability of the sinner and the autonomy of God in creating new life."[2]

Jesus reaffirms this in verse 8: "The wind blows where it wishes, and you hear its sound, but you do not know where it comes from or where it goes. So it is with everyone who is born of the Spirit." Again, Barrett comments:

> In the Greek the word for Spirit (πνεῦμα) is also wind and likewise the word for wind is also spirit. Jesus is drawing a clear parallel here between wind and Spirit (as made obvious by 3:8), so that when He speaks of one He is speaking of the other. He is comparing the effects of the wind to the effects of the Spirit. It is very important to note that the phrase the "wind blows where it wishes" conveys the

[2] Barrett, "A Scriptural Affirmation of Monergism," 155. Edwin Palmer writes: "In birth a baby is completely helpless. He does not make himself. He is made. He is born. There is complete passivity on his part. Obviously a baby could not have said to his parents before he was born, 'I determine that I shall be born.' And so it is in the case of spiritual birth. That which is not yet born cannot say, 'I will to be born.' That which is dead spiritually cannot say, 'I will to live.' And that which has not yet been created cannot say, 'I will to be created.' These are manifest impossibilities. Rather, as in the case of a baby, or creation yet to be, or a dead man, spiritual birth, creation, or life comes wholly at the discretion of the Holy Spirit. It is he who does the deciding, and not man. Man is entirely passive. The Holy Spirit is entirely sovereign, regenerating exactly whom he wills. Consequently, John could say that the children of God are 'born not of natural descent, nor of human decision or a husband's will, but born of God' (John 1:13)." Edwin H. Palmer, *The Person and Ministry of the Holy Spirit: The Traditional Calvinist Perspective* (Grand Rapids, MI: Baker, 1974), 82–83.

sovereignty of the Spirit. The Spirit is not controlled by the human will but works as God pleases to bring about new life. Therefore, a regeneration dependent upon man's will to believe or a regeneration where God and man cooperate is ruled out by the text. The Spirit's role in the new birth is sovereign because, like the wind, He works apart from human control (John 3:8; cf. John 7:37–38).[3]

Moreover, Article IV of the *BF&M* affirms this when it states:

> Regeneration, or the new birth, *is a work of God's grace* whereby believers become new creatures in Christ Jesus. It is a change of the heart *wrought by the Holy Spirit* through the conviction of sin, *to which the sinner responds* in repentance toward God and faith in the Lord Jesus Christ. *Repentance and faith are inseparable experiences of grace* (emphasis added).[4]

---

[3] Ibid., 156.

[4] Commenting on Article IV, Ascol attests: "The human action of repentance and faith are described as responsive. Ask any English professor to identify the antecedent of the pronoun 'which' and he or she will tell you that it is 'It' that began the sentence, which itself refers back to 'Regeneration, or new birth.' In other words, regeneration 'is a change of heart . . . to which the sinner responds in repentance . . . and faith. . . . This is why the BF&M goes on to confess that 'repentance and faith are inseparable experiences of *grace*' (emphasis added)" (*Traditional Theology & the SBC*, 57).

The Sovereign Work of the Father

We have already demonstrated from John 6 that salvation is unconditional and, apart from the intervening, sovereign grace of God, human beings *cannot* choose Christ (see chapter 3). John 6:44 reads: "No one can come to me unless the Father who sent me draws him. And I will raise him up on the last day." Regarding this verse, Geisler claims: "Their being drawn by God was conditioned on their faith."[5]

But is this the case? Again, the word *can* has to do with ability. The word *unless* is a necessary condition. "Coming to Jesus" (believing in Jesus) cannot happen unless the Father draws a person to the Son. This *drawing* speaks of God's irresistible grace (effectual calling)—of the Father's enabling of the sinner to come to Jesus (believe in Jesus). John 6:65 confirms this: "This is why I told you that no one can come to me unless it is granted him by the Father." The NET renders it ". . . unless the Father has allowed him to come." The NIV reads ". . . unless the Father has enabled them." Consequently, before a person can believe in Jesus, the Father must first enable him (that is, regenerate him by the work of the Holy Spirit).

This teaching is perfectly consistent throughout the corpus of John's writings. Elsewhere, the beloved

---

[5] Geisler, *Chosen But Free*, 95. In agreement with Geisler, I. H. Marshall avers: "The men whom the Father gives to Jesus are those Jews who have responded to Him" (*Kept by the Power of God*, 178).

apostle wrote "you may be sure that everyone who practices righteousness *has been* born of him" (1 John 2:29, emphasis added). A few chapters later, John makes a similar comment: "Everyone who believes that Jesus is the Christ *has been* born of God, and everyone who loves the Father loves whoever *has been* born of him" (1 John 5:1, emphasis added). Notice here the verb tenses and what John is teaching. He states that the one "doing righteousness" and the one "believing" (present tense) has already been born of God (perfect tense).[6] We do not first believe so that we might be born again. Rather, we are first born of God so that we may believe that Jesus is the Christ. We are first regenerated in order to exercise faith and repentance in Him. Thus, regeneration precedes faith.[7]

Geisler further asserts: "It's evident that their understanding of Jesus' teaching and being drawn to [sic] the Father was accomplished through their own free will."[8] And yet, when Peter understood Jesus' true identity as the Christ, Jesus told him emphati-

[6] The perfect tense in Greek is used to describe a completed action which produced results which are still in effect up to the present.

[7] John 6:37 reads: "All that the Father gives me will come to me, and whoever comes to me I will never cast out." Note the order. Jesus does *not* say: "All who come to me the Father will give me." Thus, regeneration *precedes* faith! Commenting on John 6:43–44, Kostenberger writes: "Jesus proceeds to underscore the human inability to gain salvation apart from divine enablement. People can come to him only if the Father who sent Jesus draws them. Ultimately, therefore, salvation depends not on human believing, but on the drawing action of the Father (presumably by the Holy Spirit) by which God moves a person to faith in Christ" (*John*, 213).

[8] Geisler, *Chosen But Free*, 96.

cally: "Blessed are you, Simon Bar-Jonah! For flesh and blood has not revealed this to you, but my Father who is in heaven" (Matt. 16:17). Peter didn't come to understand this on his own—it was the gift of God the Father! Moreover, in 1 Corinthians 2:14 Paul states: "The natural person does not accept the things of the Spirit of God, for they are folly to him, and he is not able to understand them because they are spiritually discerned." Apart from sovereign grace, unregenerate man is incapable of understanding the things of God (see also 2 Cor. 4:3–4). Contra Geisler, whenever someone understands Jesus' teaching and is drawn by the Father to Jesus, it has absolutely nothing to do with "their own free will" and everything to do with the sovereign, regenerating work of God (John 1:13, 3:21; Rom. 9:16, etc.).

Sheep Before Believing

In John 10 Jesus distinguishes between the sheep and the goats. About the sheep Jesus says in vv. 3-5: "He calls his own sheep by name and leads them out. When he has brought out all his own, he goes before them, and the sheep follow him, for they know his voice." Then in vv. 14-16 Jesus says: "I am the good shepherd. I know my own and my own know me . . . and they will listen to my voice." In vv. 19–21 John tells us that the crowd was divided over Jesus and many were distressed by his teaching. Jesus aims his next words directly at them: "You do not believe because you are not among my sheep. My sheep hear my voice, and I know them, and they follow me" (vv. 26–27). Note carefully the order of Jesus' words in v. 26, paying special attention to the word *because*. According to Peterson: "Jesus implies that his hearers are either sheep or goats *before* they respond to him. . . . Their response of faith or unbelief does not *make* them either sheep or goats. Rather, their responses *show* their prior identities."[9] Regeneration precedes faith.

Election Precedes Salvation

John's Gospel also teaches that *election precedes salvation*. We learn about this in Jesus' High Priestly prayer recorded in John 17. The prayer begins in 17:1b–2: "Father, the hour has come; glorify your Son that the Son may glorify you, since you have given him authority over all flesh, to give eternal life to all whom you have given him." D. A. Carson insists: "The giving by the Father of certain men to the Son precedes their reception of eternal life, and governs the purpose of the Son's mission. There is no way to escape the implicit election."[10] Then in 17:6 Jesus says: "I have manifested your name to the people whom you gave me out of the world. Yours they were, and you gave them to me, and they have kept

[9] Peterson, *Election and Free Will*, 63.
[10] D. A. Carson, *Divine Sovereignty and Human Responsibility: Biblical Perspectives in Tension* (Grand Rapids, MI: Baker, 1994), 187.

your word." Three more times in the following vers-es Jesus refers to those whom the Father has given to Him (17:9b, 11b, 24). Clearly, election precedes sal-vation. Again, Peterson observes:

> Not once does Jesus teach that the Father gave people to him because they believe in him, because he foresaw their faith, or the like. Rather, the Father's giving a people to Jesus precedes their receiving eternal life (v. 2). And Jesus does not manifest the Father to people because they believe in him. Instead, he manifests the Father to the people whom the Father gave him, and as a result they re-ceive Jesus' words and believe that the Father sent him (vv. 6–8). That is, *the Father does not give them to the Son because they believe, but they believe because the Father gave them to the Son* (emphasis added).[11]

Even Our Faith Is a Gift

The biblical concept that regeneration precedes faith seems illogical until we begin to grasp the depth of human depravity. Consider Paul's teaching on the matter in Ephesians 2:1–9:

> And you were dead in the trespasses and sins in which you once walked, following the

[11] Peterson, *Election and Free Will*, 65.

course of this world, following the prince of the power of the air, the spirit that is now at work in the sons of disobedience—among whom we all once lived in the passions of our flesh, carrying out the desires of the body and the mind, and were by nature children of wrath, like the rest of mankind. But God, being rich in mercy, because of the great love with which he loved us, even when we were dead in our trespasses, made us alive together with Christ—by grace you have been saved—and raised us up with him and seated us with him in the heavenly places in Christ Jesus, so that in the coming ages he might show the immeasurable riches of his grace in kindness toward us in Christ Jesus. For by grace you have been saved through faith. And this is not your own doing; it is the gift of God, not a result of works, so that no one may boast.

Twice in this passage Paul says that in our unregenerate state we were spiritually dead (vv. 1, 5). Not spiritually weak, but *dead*! Question: What can a dead man do? *Absolutely nothing*! No wonder Paul speaks in this passage about God raising the spiritually dead to life. In verse 5 we read that God "made us alive together with Christ," and in verse 6 that He "raised us up with him and seated us with him in the heavenly places in Christ Jesus." Paul presents us with a glaring contrast here. Man is spiritually dead;

he can do absolutely nothing about his spiritual condition. Notice verse 4: "But God . . ." Only God can raise the dead—and *this* is grace! "This" refers to the entire process of salvation—including our faith.[12] Thus, even our *faith* is a gift of God's grace. As Davis declares:

> Ephesians 2:9 is a heat-seeking missile heading directly for the heart of the doctrine of election based on foreseen faith. For such a view relies on the conception of faith as something resident in the heart of man which he then uses to lift himself up out of the common muck of human rebellion so that Christ can save him. But if faith is not from ourselves but is a specific gift of God to the elect, then all boasting is excluded.[13]

Non-Calvinists object, insisting that if faith is the gift of God then it cannot be a genuine response of the individual. For example, in 2012 the "Statement of Traditional Southern Baptists Understanding of the Plan of Salvation" was published by a group of non-Calvinist Southern Baptist leaders.[14] Article XIII of that document reads in part: "We deny that the

---

[12] As Sproul attests: "Grammatically, the antecedent of 'this' includes the word 'faith'" (*Everyone's A Theologian*, 228).

[13] Davis, "Unconditional Election," 60.

[14] According to Ascol, this document was published "in order to assert their doctrinal convictions vis-à-vis the resurgence of the doctrines of grace . . . within the SBC" (*Traditional Theology & the SBC*, 7).

decision of faith is an act of God rather than a response of the person." In response to this statement, Ascol argues:

> If by "decision of faith" the authors mean the act of trusting Christ, then of course it is not "an act of God." God does not believe for anyone. Sinners are those who must believe on the Lord Jesus in order to be saved. It is the individual's faith, not God's. . . . Who in the SBC suggests otherwise? However, giving the authors the benefit of the doubt, I suspect they are primarily concerned to reject the idea that faith is the gift of God. In their scheme if this is true then faith cannot be a genuine response of the individual. Scripture, however, teaches that it is both (Ephesians 2:8-9; Philippians 1:29; Acts 16:32, etc.).[15]

Likewise, Boice and Ryken clarify the matter when they write:

> The immediate effect of the divine regeneration of the soul is that the sinner now abhors the sin that he once cherished, and trusts in Christ for his salvation. This involves two actions: 1) turning from sin, which is repentance; and 2) turning to Christ, which is faith. These are both things that we do. That is,

[15] Ibid., 69.

God does not repent for us, nor does he believe for us. We must repent. We must believe. Nevertheless, both repentance and faith occur in us because of God's prior work of regeneration.[16]

Moreover, it should be noted that Article X on "Regeneration" of the *Abstract of Principles* affirms this doctrine:

> Saving faith is the belief, on God's authority, of whatsoever is revealed in His Word concerning Christ; accepting and resting upon Him alone for justification and eternal life. *It is wrought in the heart by the Holy Spirit*, and is accompanied by all other saving graces, and leads to a life of holiness (emphasis mine).

That No One May Boast

Regeneration precedes faith. Consequently, God gets *all* of the glory for our salvation, thus stripping us of our ability to boast (Eph. 2:8–9). If this order (regeneration before faith) seems illogical to us, perhaps it is due to our having too high a view of fallen humanity, on the one hand, and too low a view of God's sovereignty, on the other. Which view exalts God's grace more and leaves no room for boasting whatsoever: the Calvinist or non-Calvinist view?

[16] Boice and Ryken, *The Doctrines of Grace*, 149–150.

We conclude with some sobering remarks by John Murray regarding John 3:3–8:

> It has often been said that we are passive in regeneration. This is a true and proper statement. For it is simply the precipitate of what our Lord has taught us here. We may not like it. We may recoil against it. It may not fit into our way of thinking and it may not accord with the timeworn expressions which are the coin of our evangelism. But if we recoil against it, we do well to remember that this recoil is recoil against Christ. And what shall we answer when we appear before him whose truth we rejected and with whose gospel we tampered? But blessed be God that the gospel of Christ is one of sovereign, efficacious, irresistible regeneration. If it were not the case that in regeneration we are passive, the subjects of an action of which God alone is the agent, there would be no gospel at all. For unless God by sovereign, operative grace had turned our enmity to love and our disbelief to faith we would never yield the response of faith and love.[17]

[17] John Murray, *Redemption Accomplished and Applied* (Grand Rapids, MI: Eerdmans, 1955), 99–100.

7

Does God Love Everyone Equally?

Calvinists do not deny that God is all-loving. After all, love is an attribute of God. God loves—that is His nature! The pertinent question is, does God love everyone *equally*? The short answer is *no*, God does *not* love everyone equally—not according to the Bible. Let me explain.

A God Who Discriminates

God loves the Son in a way that is different from His love for creation (Matt. 3:17; John 3:35; 5:20). God's love for Israel was different than His love for Israel's neighbors (Deut. 7:6–10, 10:15, 14:2; Ps. 147:19; Amos 3:2; Rom. 9:4–5). God's love for Jacob was different than His love for Esau (Gen. 25:23; Rom. 9:12–13). God's love for Isaac was different than His love for Ishmael (Gen. 21:10; Gal. 4:30). And God's love for the Church is different than His love for the world—just as a father may love "all the children of the world," but he loves his own biological children with a different, special kind of love (John 13:1; 17:9, 26; Eph. 5:25, 29). If we humans can discriminate and differentiate in expressing love, why should we not think God can do likewise? Should we suppose we are greater than God in being able to manifest different kinds of love? Certainly not. It is obvious that God does not love everyone *equally*. As Packer attests:

> God loves all in some ways (everyone whom he creates, sinners though they are, receives many undeserved good gifts in daily providence), and . . . he loves some in all ways (that is, in addition to the gifts of daily providence he brings them to faith, to new life, and to glory according to his predestinating purpose). This is the clear witness of the entire Bible.[1]

When Packer states that "God loves us all in some ways," he is referring to *common grace*. Jesus spoke of this kind of grace in Matthew 5:45 when He said that God "makes his sun rise on the evil and on the good, and sends rain on the just and on the unjust." This is to be distinguished from *special grace*, which

---

[1] J. I. Packer, "The Love of God: Universal and Particular" in *Still Sovereign: Contemporary Perspectives on Election, Foreknowledge, & Grace* (Grand Rapids, MI: Baker, 2000), 283–284.

pertains to salvation. Packer refers to special grace when he says that "God loves some in all ways." That is, God shows common grace to everyone; but God shows common grace *and* special grace only to some. God does not treat all people *equally*.

There are distinctives in God's love. Throughout the Bible we see a God who *discriminates*. God chose Abraham (Gen. 12:1–3; 18:19) when he was steeped in paganism (Josh. 24:2). Are we to imagine that Abraham somehow lifted himself out of this morally corrupt environment by his own willpower? No, it was sheer grace that God revealed Himself to Abraham and chose him out of the mass of idolatrous humanity. In Luke 1:15 we read that John the Baptist "was filled with the Holy Spirit, even from his mother's womb." That was certainly not my experience. I am guessing it was not yours either. And, I dare say, it sounds like discrimination to me. But, of course, that is God's prerogative!

In Acts 9:1–19 we read that Saul was hell-bent on destroying the Christian faith. He was certainly *not* seeking Christ. But Christ, in His mercy, stopped Saul dead in his tracks and turned him around one hundred and eighty degrees in the opposite direction. Non-Calvinists may reply: "Yes, but this was an unusual case since Saul was called to take the gospel to the Gentiles." There is no denying that fact. But neither is there any denying that God chose Saul for salvation too. Saul's conversion was all of God! But here's the thing: If God wanted to He *could* save *everyone* the way He saved Saul (by sovereign grace, the way anyone is saved). But clearly He does not. The God of the Bible is a God who discriminates.[2]

God Did Not Plan To Save *Everyone*

Does God really want to save *every single person*? If so, then why throughout history has God left so many of the nations in the dark when He could have given them the light? Millions of pagans who lived during Old Testament times knew little or nothing about the law of Moses or the promised Messiah. Moreover, in John 12:32 Jesus said: "And I, when I am lifted up from the earth, will draw all people to myself." Did Jesus literally mean *all* people without exception? Or did He perhaps mean *all sorts of people without distinction* (Rev. 5:9)? If Jesus literally meant all people, then what are we to make of the millions down through the centuries who never heard the gospel? What do we make of the millions

---

[2] In his book *Chosen But Free*, Geisler asserts that if Calvinism is true, then God is not all-loving. In response, James White writes: "The single most fundamental rebuttal of this erroneous argument is simply this: *Arminians should well consider why they demand that God have less freedom in His actions and His love than they grant to the creature man.* . . . The key problem with Geisler's attack is that it demands that God's love be indiscriminate. While man has the freedom to love those closest to him with a particular love that is not given to anyone else, God is not granted this freedom. If He is to be 'all loving' then His love is to have no distinctions, no freedom, no particularity. Love all the same or love none at all is the argument." James R. White, *The Potter's Freedom: A Defense of the Reformation and a Rebuttal of Norman Geisler's Chosen But Free* (Amityville, NY: Calvary Press Publishing, 2000), 303.

today who have yet to hear the gospel? If they die in that lost state, will they perish? This is how Paul described the spiritual state of his Gentile readers *before* they heard and believed the gospel: "Remember that you were at that time separated from Christ, alienated from the commonwealth of Israel and strangers to the covenants of promise, having no hope and without God in the world" (Eph. 2:12).

Pluralism is the view that all religious paths are valid and therefore all paths lead to God. *Inclusivism* is the view that people may be saved (by the Person and work of Jesus) without consciously hearing the gospel or believing in Jesus. *Exclusivism* is the view that Jesus is the *only* path to God and that conscious knowledge of and personal faith in Jesus are *necessary* for salvation. Now, unless we embrace pluralism or inclusivism, we must admit that those who die apart from conscious faith in Jesus Christ will perish (John 14:6; Acts 4:12; Rom. 10:14, etc.). Of course, as Christians, our hearts should break over the lostness of humanity. But the point I am trying to make is that *God's plan has never been to save every single human being on the planet.* Both the Bible and missions history confirm this.

Why have some countries received the light of the gospel and others have not? One could argue that this is on us—our own failure to take the mandate we have been given seriously (Matt. 28:18–20). I do not doubt that we should take this mandate more seriously. But where does God's sovereignty fit into the picture? God determines where, when, and how the gospel goes forth (Acts 16:6–10). Yet, I have personally known of missionaries who were ready to take the gospel to the nations, but the door never opened for them. We must acknowledge that, since "salvation is of the Lord" (Jonah 2:9), God is sovereign over missions! Revelation 3:7 applies here. There, Jesus said that He is the one "who opens and no one will shut, who shuts and no one opens."

Even in America today we must admit that things are not equal. The very fact that some are privileged to grow up in a loving Christian home environment who are exposed to the gospel regularly while others are not is ample proof that God does not subscribe to this notion of equality that many insist on His behalf. Should this inequality of opportunity merely be chalked up to good fortune or to coincidence? If so, then God is not sovereign. Where does God's providence fit into the picture? Orrick observes:

> God is in control of when and where people
> are born. He planned for you to be born in a
> place and time such that you would hear the
> gospel. The same day that you were born,
> thousands of other people were born who
> might never hear the name of Jesus one time
> in their lives. Is this fair?[3]

---

[3] Orrick, *Mere Calvinism*, 60.

Personally, whenever I consider this, I cannot help but humbly thank my God for His merciful providence in my life. Those who suggest this theology of God's sovereignty, and its logical outworkings, results in reasons for mankind to boast do not grasp the reality of that truth and have not properly come to terms with the reality that salvation is foremost and primarily for God's own glory and honor. We stand in awe and express a humble attitude from the depths of our hearts when we truly realize that we are among the precious few to whom God has graciously chosen to reveal the glorious truths leading to salvation. That sobering thought alone should arrest any delusion of human insistence upon divine fairness and equality, as if God is obligated to His own creation. But I digress.

Let us probe even deeper. Why do some people believe in the Lord Jesus Christ and others do not? If *you* are a believer in Jesus Christ, then why do *you* believe in Jesus and your unbelieving neighbor does not (though perhaps he/she will in time)? Are you more intelligent or somehow more spiritually astute than they are? Was it because of something *you* saw, realized, or did? Or was it because God, in His mercy, opened your blinded eyes, gave you understanding, and drew you to Himself (2 Cor. 4:3–6)? What really makes you different than your unbelieving neighbor? Did you make yourself to differ? No, left to yourself you would never have chosen to follow

Christ on your own. It is all of grace (1 Cor. 4:7).

Non-Calvinists Are Not Off the Hook

A common objection made by non-Calvinists runs along these lines: "If God has the power to save anyone He wants even against their will, but everyone doesn't get saved, then God doesn't desire for everyone to get saved." When you stop and think about it though, non-Calvinists are not off the hook here. Calvinists might just as well ask non-Calvinists: "Since God *has* the power to save everyone, why doesn't He do it?" Non-Calvinists may reply: "God allowed Adam and Eve to be tempted by Satan because genuine love requires *freedom of choice*." In other words, true freedom exists only when one is able to choose between two options from a posture of neutrality and without any bias. But as we saw in chapter 3, this will not work. First of all, God is the most free Being that exists. In fact, God has *absolute* freedom. And yet, He cannot even be tempted to do evil. Second, the saints in heaven are as free to love God as they have ever been or ever will be, and yet the option of choosing against God is impossible— yet we all agree they are free agents who make volitional choices.

Furthermore, Calvinists might also ask non-Calvinists: "Why did God create Satan, knowing that he would rebel against Him and tempt Adam and Eve to do likewise? Why did God allow the Fall to happen, knowing that many would perish for all eternity as a result of it?"[4] No, non-Calvinists are definitely not off the hook when it comes to this issue.

Let's Talk About *Fairness*

Non-Calvinists will often assert: "If God did not love everyone equally, then God would not be fair!" It just so happens that Paul addresses this issue in that much debated chapter 9 of his letter to the Romans. Let us examine what Paul teaches there. Romans 9:6–13 says:

> But it is not as though the word of God has failed. For not all who are descended from Israel belong to Israel, and not all are children of Abraham because they are his offspring, but "Through Isaac shall your offspring be named." This means that it is not the children of the flesh who are the children of God, but the children of the promise are counted as offspring. For this is what the promise said:

[4] White argues: "In Geisler's view, God *wants* to save every single person, *but is incapable of doing so*. He loves every single individual equally, but, despite this love and all that He has done to save every person, millions perish. One could easily argue that a God that would create a universe well knowing that in the final outcome millions of the objects of His love would end up in eternal punishment and all His best efforts would be frustrated would not be considered a very wise or, a very loving God. Why create, and set His love upon, creatures that He knows, infallibly, will destroy themselves in rebellion and will thwart His every effort to save them?" (*The Potter's Freedom*, 304).

"About this time next year I will return, and Sarah shall have a son." And not only so, but also when Rebekah had conceived children by one man, our forefather Isaac, though they were not yet born and had done nothing either good or bad– in order that God's purpose of election might continue, not because of works but because of him who calls— she was told, "The older will serve the younger." As it is written, "Jacob I loved, but Esau I hated."[5]

In Romans 9:11–13 Paul says that God chose Jacob and rejected Esau "though they were not yet born and had done nothing either good or bad." Note that God's choice was not based on foreseen faith, but rather "in order that God's purpose of election might continue." Furthermore, it was "not because of works but because of him who calls." Geisler alleges: "Few scriptural texts are more misused than this one. . . . God is not speaking here about the *individual* Jacob but about the *nation* of Jacob (Israel)."[6] He then cites Genesis 25:23 as proof: "Two nations are in your womb, and two peoples from within you shall be divided; the one shall be stronger than the other, the older shall serve the younger."

To be sure, Paul may very well be thinking of Ja-

---

[5] Sproul notes: "Divine hatred is not malicious. It involves a withholding of favor" (*Chosen By God*, 149).

[6] Geisler, *Chosen But Free*, 81.

cob and Esau as representing two nations in Romans 9:11–13.[7] But even if he is, that does not negate the fact that Paul is also speaking about the salvation of individuals. In Romans 9:2–3 Paul states: "I have great sorrow and unceasing anguish in my heart. For I could wish that I myself were accursed and cut off from Christ for the sake of my brothers, my kinsmen according to the flesh" (see also Rom. 10:1). Paul's anguish is over the fact that most *individual* Jews have failed to believe in Jesus. Why then would Paul be speaking about nations here in 9:11–13? Clearly the context and the language of these verses indicate that Paul is speaking about God's election of individuals to salvation.[8]

---

[7] Had Paul wanted to communicate the idea of Jacob and Esau representing nations, it would make his argument rather strange and absurd. Are we to believe Paul is trying to say that God's choice was made before either *nation* did anything good or bad?

[8] Peterson argues: "It is right to point out that Jacob and Esau represent nations, even while within their mother's womb as the quotation of Genesis 25:23 . . . confirms. . . . But it is wrong to conclude from that fact that God fails to deal with the twins as individuals, too. . . . God deals with Jacob and Esau both as individuals and as fathers of nations. He chooses Jacob as an individual to be a special recipient of his love and chooses him to be heir of his promises to the nation. . . . The apostle is unambiguous: God chooses Jacob and rejects Esau before their birth 'in order that God's purpose in election might continue, not because of works but because of his call'" (*Election and Free Will*, 40–41). Commenting on Romans 9—11, Schreiner remarks: "[A] controversy exists over whether the salvation promised here relates to individuals or groups. . . . Such a dichotomy is logically and exegetically flawed, for groups are always composed of individuals, and one cannot have the former without including the latter. . . . The selection of a remnant out of Israel implies the selection of some individuals out of a larger group. Moreover, the unity of Romans 9—11 indicates that individual election cannot be eliminated. In chapter 10 believing in Jesus is an individual decision, even though large groups of Gentiles are doing so. The individual and corporate dimensions cannot be sundered from one another in

Not only this, but note carefully what Paul says next:

> What shall we say then? Is there injustice on God's part? By no means! For he says to Moses, "I will have mercy on whom I have mercy, and I will have compassion on whom I have compassion." So then it depends not on human will or exertion, but on God, who has mercy (Rom. 9:14–16).

It is evident from verse 14 that Paul anticipates that some of his readers will object to this teaching. One thing is for certain, however: Paul's readers would *not* have objected to God's choice of Israel (represented by Jacob) over Edom (represented by Esau) or any other nation for that matter. For one thing, the church in Rome consisted mostly of Jews, who were steeped in the Old Testament teaching that they were God's chosen people (Deut. 7:6, 14:2; Pss. 105:43; 135:4).

But even Gentiles had for many centuries believed "the gods" favored one nation over another. Consequently, Gentile converts who had embraced Jesus as

chapter 10, and the same principle applies to chapter 9. . . . Those who insist that corporate election alone is intended in chapters 9 and 11 are inconsistent when they revert to individual decisions of faith in chapter 10. The three chapters must be interpreted together, yielding the conclusion that both corporate and individual election are involved." Thomas R. Schreiner, *Romans* in Baker Exegetical Commentary on the New Testament, ed. Moisés Silva (Grand Rapids, MI: Baker Academic, 1998), 497–498.

the fulfillment of the Old Testament Messianic prophecies, would likewise have embraced the Old Testament teaching that Israel was God's chosen people. Therefore, no one in the church at Rome, Jew or Gentile, would have objected to God's choosing one nation over another. That was *not* the issue here. So what was the issue? *God's choosing one individual over another individual for salvation—the same issue that non-Calvinists object to today!*[9] For example, former president of the SBC and non-Calvinist, Frank Page, makes the following assertion:

> Perhaps one of the most often used (or abused) passages in regards to election is Romans 9. Please note that election is *not* God choosing or electing some to be saved and some to be lost. In fact, to say that is charging God with doing something that He cannot do, because He has provided salvation for every human being who would receive and accept it.[10]

Calvinists do not deny that God has "promised salvation for every human being who would receive

---

[9] Davis attests: "The Arminian view of election based on foreseen faith would not cause such a reaction. But Paul knew that the doctrine he was teaching—of unconditional election based solely on the sovereignty of God––would cause the sense of outrage that Wesley articulated centuries later" ("Unconditional Election," 55). In a sermon titled "Divine Sovereignty" (No. 77, Vol. 2), C. H. Spurgeon declared: "No doctrine . . . has more excited the hatred of mankind than the truth of the absolute sovereignty of God."

[10] Page, *Trouble with the Tulip*, 63.

and accept it." As it stands, this simply affirms the universal offer of the gospel. However, Calvinists vehemently reject Page's assertion that unconditional election is something "that He cannot do." According to Romans 9:15–16, this is exactly what God Himself says he actually *does*.[11] In anticipation of his readers objecting to this difficult doctrine, Paul asks: "Is there injustice on God's part?" (v. 14). In other words, "Wouldn't that mean God is *unfair*?" Paul answers the question emphatically: "By no means!" Orrick is surely right when he insists:

> We need to revise our understanding of what constitutes fairness. Fairness does not consist in treating everyone equally; fairness consists in giving everyone what he deserves. . . . One of the fundamental principles in Scripture is that God is not obligated to show mercy to anyone. And if he is not obligated to show mercy to anyone, then he cannot be unfair if he shows mercy to no one. How then is it unfair if he shows mercy to only one person, or to only one nation, or to as many as he chooses?[12]

[11] Orrick declares: "When you see that the Lord has revealed something about himself and the way he acts, even if it is something that contradicts or challenges your long-cherished ideas about who God is, do not deflect the truth by saying, 'My God is not like that' or 'My God would never do that.' If the Bible asserts something about God to be true, and it could not possibly be true of *your* God, then you have the wrong God" *Mere Calvinism*, 16.

[12] Ibid., 62.

Non-Calvinist Proof Texts

Before we conclude the chapter, let us consider a few proof texts often cited by non-Calvinists ostensibly to "prove" that God loves everyone equally. Each of the following three biblical texts speak of God's love for "the world":

> For God so loved the world, that he gave his only Son, that whoever believes in him should not perish but have eternal life (John 3:16).

> My little children, I am writing these things to you so that you may not sin. But if anyone does sin, we have an advocate with the Father, Jesus Christ the righteous. He is the propitiation for our sins, and not for ours only but also for the sins of the whole world (1 John 2:1–2).

> Beloved, let us love one another, for love is from God, and whoever loves has been born of God and knows God. Anyone who does not love does not know God, because God is love. In this the love of God was made manifest among us, that God sent his only Son into the world, so that we might live through him (1 John 4:7–9).

In chapter 4 we saw that in the Bible the word "all" does not always mean *everyone without exception*.

The same applies when it comes to the use of the word "world" in the Bible. Gatiss comments:

> When it comes to the word "world," the most important texts to consider are John 1:29, John 3:16, and 1 John 2:2. . . . It is unnecessary to claim that κόσμος (*kosmos*, world) here means "a world within the world," such as "the elect" or "the church." . . . Yet it is also unwarranted to simply assume it means "everyone on the planet" without regard for the context. John specifically distinguishes disciples from the world (e.g., John 14:17, 15:18, 17:9), thus showing that even within the Gospel itself the term "world" cannot mean everyone without exception. . . . As for John 3:16, when examined carefully it does not actually say anything at all about the extent or intent of the atonement directly. In a sense, it is irrelevant to the argument. What John 3:16 is talking about is God's motivation in sending Jesus into the (darkness-loving, God-hating) world to die. He did it because he did not want to give up on humanity as a whole . . . but it is not about "a purpose to save every person in the world individually." It also speaks about the universal offer and invitation of the gospel which is not the same as . . . universal atonement. It does not say that God set out to save every single person in

the world or that Christ "died for" every single person in the world. It does, however, widen out the scope of God's love which is wide enough to embrace not just Israel but the world. God so loved the rebellious world that he provided a way for rebellious sinners to be saved through Christ. *Anyone* who believes in him will not perish. He is given to the world in such a way that everyone who believes is saved.[13]

In light of this interpretive framework, passages such as John 3:16, 1 John 2:1–2 and 1 John 4:7–9, etc., must likewise be interpreted in view of the whole of Scripture. In chapter 4, I stated that one of the primary reasons I am a Calvinist is because I am convinced that the Calvinist hermeneutic (i.e., approach to interpreting Scripture) is far better at harmonizing Scripture than the non-Calvinist approach.[14] This is a case in point. Many an SBC church today identifies itself as being "a John 3:16 church." In recent years a group of non-Calvinist

[13] Gatiss, *For Us and For Our Salvation*, 47–49. Regarding John 3:16–17, Orrick notes: "The Jews sometimes referred to the non-Jews as *the world*, and it was commonly assumed that when Messiah came, he would condemn *the world*" (*Mere Calvinism*, 102).

[14] Sproul's comments cited in footnote 4 on p. 43 are here worth repeating: "Reformed theology is systematic. The science of systematic theology is so called because it attempts to understand doctrine in a coherent and unified manner. It is not the goal of systematic theology to impose on the Bible a system derived from a particular philosophy. Rather, its goal is to discern the interrelatedness of the teachings of Scripture itself" (*What Is Reformed Theology?*, 23).

Southern Baptists (who prefer to be called "Traditionalists") founded a ministry called *Connect 316* to promote their so-called "traditionalist" view of salvation. Although there may be some, I don't know of a single Calvinistic church or parachurch ministry that identifies itself in this way. I know of no Reformed SBC churches that identify as being a "John 6:44 church" or a "Romans 9:15 church." But I am aware of *many* such churches and ministries that stress the importance of preaching "the whole counsel of God" (Acts 20:27). We are not to interpret the Bible through the lens of John 3:16. Rather, we are to read John 3:16 in view of the whole of Scripture, and interpreting Scripture with Scripture. Only then can we understand and interpret John 3:16 in a way that harmonizes with the whole of Scripture.[15]

---

[15] According to Spurgeon: "Arminianism is guilty of confusing doctrines and acting as an obstruction to a clear and lucid grasp of the Scripture; because it misstates or ignores the eternal purpose of God, it dislocates the meaning of the whole plan of redemption. Indeed, confusion is inevitable apart from this foundational truth [of election]. Without it there is a lack of unity of thought, and generally speaking they have no idea whatever of a system of divinity. It is almost impossible to make a man a theologian unless you begin with this [doctrine of election]. You may if you please put a young believer to college for years, but unless you shew him this ground-plan of the everlasting covenant, he will make little progress, because his studies do not cohere, he does not see how one truth fits with another, and how all truths must harmonize together." Charles Spurgeon, "Effects of Sound Doctrine," sermon delivered on Sunday evening, April 22, 1860, at New Park Street Chapel.

8

Who's Responsible for Unbelief?

If indeed God elects unconditionally those who will ultimately be saved, does He also elect some to eternal damnation? In other words, does God work equally in the lives of both the elect and the non-elect: working faith in the former to insure their salvation, and unbelief in the latter to insure their damnation (a view known as *equal ultimacy*)? And if so, does that not make God responsible for man's unbelief?

No Symmetry Here!

The answer is, absolutely not; there is no symmetry here! God does *not* create unbelief in the non-elect. That unbelief is already there due to their fallen nature.[1] Ascol explains:

---

[1] Ascol observes: "Does God work in the same way to 'cause' a person to reject Christ? Absolutely not. People are born rejecting Christ because they

> Election is the beginning of [God's] rescue
> mission. It is the first step in His work to in-
> sure the salvation of sinners. He does not act
> in a symmetrical way with those whom He
> does not elect. That is, He does not "elect
> them to hell." They are already on the way to
> hell. God simply leaves them "to act in their
> sin to their just condemnation."[2]

The phrase "to act in their sin to their just condemnation" is from the *Philadelphia Baptist Confession* (1742).[3] People do not go to hell because God
elected them for that. That's not what Reformed
theology teaches. Rather, people go to hell because
they are, first and foremost, radically corrupt sinners
who innately loathe God. Don't forget the harsh criticism Paul laid out in Romans 3 where he said every
single person is by nature sinful to their core as a
consequence from the fall of our first parents, Adam
and Eve. And because of this very real and personal
sin, it means there are no morally-neutral beings.
Quite the opposite. It is out of those non-seekers that
He chooses to show mercy to some while passing
over others, allowing them to remain in their own

are by nature children of wrath (Ephesians 2:3). God is no less sovereign
over those who reject Christ than those who trust Him savingly, but the
only way a person stops rejecting Christ and begins to trust Him is through
the sovereign, gracious work of God in his or her life." (*Traditional
Theology & the SBC*, 68).

[2] Ibid., 61.

[3] See pp. 12–13.

state in which they freely and contentedly dwell apart from Him. This is how R. C. Sproul has expressed it:

> The Reformed view teaches that God positively or actively intervenes in the lives of the elect to insure their salvation. The rest of mankind God leaves to themselves. He does not create unbelief in their hearts. That unbelief is already there. He does not coerce them to sin. They sin by their own choices. In the Calvinist view the decree of election is positive; the decree of reprobation is negative.[4]

According to W. S. Reid, the term *reprobation* "refers to the fact that God has condemned the nonelect to eternal punishment for their sins."[5] But again, there is no symmetry here. As Boice and Ryken maintain: "In election God actively intervenes to rescue those who deserve destruction, whereas in reprobation God passively allows some to receive the just punishment they deserve for their sins."[6] Consequently, man alone is responsible for his unbelief, and his condemnation is just. Why is mankind's con-

---

[4] Sproul, *Chosen By God*, 142–143.

[5] W. S. Reid, "Reprobation" in *Evangelical Dictionary of Theology*, Second Edition, Ed. Walter A. Elwell (Grand Rapids, MI: Baker, 1999), 1012. Reid further states: "Calvin himself set forth this doctrine very clearly and precisely in his *Institutes* ... and while he regarded it as a dreadful doctrine, he denied that it was to be avoided or rejected, for it is clearly taught in the Scriptures" (Ibid., 1012–1013).

[6] Boice and Ryken, 104.

demnation just? It boils down to this: God said so. He made the rules. He exercises His divine prerogatives as Maker and Ruler of the universe. He has revealed how it is that one may dwell eternally with Him, and He alone decides what is required of us, created beings responsible solely to Him. Those who fail to live up to these standards have no standing to accuse God of not electing them to salvation. Mankind freely and willfully choose to sin and have no inclination toward God as He has revealed Himself. Even those people who are outwardly religious, yet fail to submit to the one true God, despise Yahweh and instead long for a god after their own imaginations.

God Hardens Whomever He Wills

In the previous chapter we examined Romans 9:6–16. In this chapter we will examine Romans 9:17–24. We will begin with vv. 17–18:

> For the Scripture says to Pharaoh, "For this very purpose I have raised you up, that I might show my power in you, and that my name might be proclaimed in all the earth." So then he has mercy on whomever he wills, and he hardens whomever he wills.

Regarding verse 18, we must ask how is it exactly that God "hardens whomever he wills"? According to Sproul:

> All that God needs to do to harden the heart
> of a person whose heart is already desperately
> wicked is to "give him over to his sin" . . .
> [and] to remove the restraints. . . . Rather
> than restricting their human freedom, he in-
> creases it. . . . It is not that God puts his hand
> on them to create fresh evil in their hearts; he
> merely removes his holy hand of restraint
> from them and lets them do their own will.[7]

This vital truth is found throughout the Bible and
is one that cannot be overlooked when discussing
this point. One place where this truth is clearly
taught is Roman 1:18–32. There Paul tells us that
God's wrath is being revealed against all human beings who suppress the truth of God and give themselves over to idolatry. As a result, Paul says, "God
gave them up" (vv. 24, 26, 28). That is to say, God
removed the restraints, their sin increased, and their
hearts grew harder. *This* is how God "hardens
whomever he wills" and not by compelling otherwise
morally upright people to commit evil.[8]

---

[7] Sproul, *Chosen by God*, 144–145.

[8] Incidentally, the truth being suppressed here is not God's *special revela-*
tion (what is known about God through the Gospel), but rather, God's *gen-*
eral revelation (what is known about God through the natural world). Paul
says the suppression of this light about God's nature and power revealed
through the natural world renders them "without excuse" and deserving of
God's just wrath. This rules out the possibility of inclusivism (see p. 85).
Paul makes it very clear that "no one seeks after God" (Rom. 3:11) and that

Paul is clearly teaching this same truth in Romans 9:17–18. Again, God did not have to "create fresh evil in [Pharaoh's] heart," as Sproul puts it. Rather, God "merely removed his holy hand of restraint" from Pharaoh and left him to his own sinful desires. God increased Pharaoh's freedom to do as he pleased. Consequently, Pharaoh's sin increased and his heart simultaneously grew harder. It was a downward spiral that ultimately led to his eternal destruction. *This* is how God hardened Pharaoh's heart. And *this* is how God "hardens whomever he wills."[9]

Mercy on Display through Wrath

In v. 19 Paul anticipates another objection from some of his readers: "You will say to me then, 'Why does he still find fault? For who can resist his will?'" In other words, "Since God's will is irresistible, how can God hold man responsible?" Non-Calvinists will

---

"the whole world [is] held accountable to God" (Rom. 3:19).

[9] According to Horton: "God is not active in hardening hearts in the same way that he is active in softening hearts. Scripture does speak of God hardening hearts, not only in Exodus 7:3 and Romans 9:18 but also in Joshua 11:20; John 12:40; Romans 11:7; 2 Corinthians 3:14. Yet it also speaks of sinners hardening their own hearts (Ex. 8:15; Ps. 95:8; Isa. 63:17; Matt. 19:8; Heb. 3:8, 13). No passage speaks of sinners softening their own hearts and regenerating themselves. Human beings are alone responsible for their hardness of heart, but God alone softens and in fact re-creates the hearts of his elect (1 Kings 8:58; Ps. 51:10; Isa. 57:15; Jer. 31:31-34; Ezek. 11:19; 36:26; 2 Cor. 3:3; 4:6; Heb 10:16). In short, God only has to leave us to our own devices in the case of reprobation, but it requires the greatest works of the triune God to save the elect, including the death of the Father's only begotten Son" (*For* Calvinism, 57–58).

never have to deal with this objection—but Paul sure did![10] His reply? Verse 20: "But who are you, O man, to answer back to God? Will what is molded say to its molder, 'Why have you made me like this?'" Commenting on this verse, Peterson writes:

> If the Arminian understanding of predestination were correct, here would have been an ideal place for Paul to say so: "Your objection shows that you have misunderstood me. I do not mean that God utterly controls salvation. Rather, he always takes our free will into account. Election means that he ratifies our choice of him. If we did not have a part, it would be unjust of God to still find fault with us. If we cannot resist the will of the Almighty, then he treats us unfairly." But Paul says none of this. Instead, he puts us in our place, far below the high and holy, great and awesome, sovereign and incomprehensible God. . . . Paul teaches that . . . human beings . . . have no ultimate right to hold him accountable to our understanding of eternal things. No, it is he—almighty God—who holds us accountable. It is he—not puny human beings—who has the ultimate say in matters of eternal destinies.[11]

---

[10] Orrick asserts: "If your version of election does not sound unjust to the natural man, it is almost certainly not the version of election we have here in Romans 9" (*Mere Calvinism*, 71).

[11] Peterson, *Election and Free Will*, 119.

The bottom line is that God does not owe us an answer. He is the Sovereign Lord, and He does as He pleases! It is only when we first approach this topic from a man-centered standpoint and insist salvation is all about us that we reach conclusions about unfairness and God holding us accountable. Again, had we properly understood that salvation is foremost and primarily about the Triune God and the glory it brings to Him, then all such objections would immediately vanish. If we find ourselves on the wrong side of this objection, if we discover that we are making the *same objection* as the imaginary interlocutor Paul anticipates, we must ask ourselves how we can continue in our grumbling against God. It should compel us to reexamine our thought process and reevaluate our objections to this doctrine.

Not yet done, Paul continues in vv. 21–24:

> Has the potter no right over the clay, to make out of the same lump one vessel for honorable use and another *for* dishonorable use? What if God, desiring to show his wrath and to make known his power, has endured with much patience vessels of wrath prepared for destruction, in order to make known the riches of his glory for vessels of mercy, which he has prepared beforehand for glory—even us whom he has called, not from the Jews only but also from the Gentiles? (emphasis added).

Paul's central point is that God's mercy is on display through His justified wrath against sin; that is, God's mercy shines all the more against the backdrop of His righteous anger against defilements of His law. In other words, we would surely fail to appreciate God's mercy if we did not also see God's wrath being displayed. As Schreiner puts it: "The mercy of God would not be impressed on the consciousness of human beings apart from the exercise of God's wrath, just as one delights more richly in the warmth, beauty, and tenderness of spring after one has experienced the cold blast of winter."[12]

There Is No Injustice Here!

Nevertheless, as in Paul's day, so today many find this teaching intolerable because it contradicts their sense of *fairness*. But this should not be the case since there is no injustice here. Note carefully that "the clay" with which God ("the Potter") works is fallen, rebellious humanity. This entire mass of unregener-

---

[12] Schreiner, *Romans*, 523. According to Edwards: "The glory of God is the greatest good; it is that which is the chief end of creation; it is of greater importance than anything else. But this is one way wherein God will glorify himself as in the eternal destruction of ungodly men he will glorify his justice. . . . God hereby directly glorifies his grace on the vessels of mercy. . . . Hereby the saints will be made more sensible how great their salvation is." Jonathan Edwards, "The Eternity of Hell Torments" in *The Torments of Hell: Jonathan Edwards on Eternal Damnation*, ed. William C. Nichols (Ames, IA: International Outreach, 2006), 126. Orrick contends: "What God did to Pharaoh is a picture of what he has been doing throughout the history of the world. He patiently endures the non-elect for the purpose of making his glory and mercy known to those he has called—the elect" (*Mere Calvinism*, 72–73).

ate humanity stands guilty before God and is deserving of His just condemnation (Rom. 3:19b). Horton rightly claims:

> The "whole lump" is guilty and corrupt. It is not a neutral lump of clay, but a condemned mass. God is not arbitrarily choosing some and rejecting others. Rather, he is choosing some of his enemies for salvation and leaving the rest to the destiny that all of us would have chosen for ourselves.[13]

There is no injustice here! Some receive *mercy*. Others receive *justice*. No one receives *injustice*. Consequently, every human being is completely responsible to the God who is absolutely sovereign over all things.

Divine Sovereignty and Human Responsibility

So how do we reconcile divine sovereignty and human responsibility? When people put this question to C. H. Spurgeon, he replied: "I never have to reconcile friends. Divine sovereignty and human responsi-

---

[13] Horton, *For Calvinism*, 57. Boice and Ryken assert: "As soon as we begin to think that God owes us something or that God *must* do something, we limit him and diminish his glory. Election and reprobation surround and protect God's glory, for they remind us that God is absolutely free and sovereign. God does whatever he wants with his universe. He is glorified in the damnation of the reprobate as well as in the salvation of the elect; his justice and his mercy are both glorious because they both demonstrate his divine sovereignty" (*The Doctrines of Grace*, 105).

bility have never had a falling out with each other. I do not need to reconcile what God has joined to-gether."[14] He further asserted: "Where these two truths meet I do not know, nor do I want to know. They do not puzzle me, since I have given up my mind to believing them both."[15]

These two doctrines run like parallel tracks throughout the Bible. On the one hand, God is abso-lutely *sovereign* in the salvation of man. On the oth-er hand, man is completely *responsible* to God for his choices and actions. This tension is especially ap-parent throughout the Gospel of John. Space forbids us to survey this teaching in John's Gospel, so we will limit our study to John 3:14–21. Let's begin with vv. 14–18:

> And as Moses lifted up the serpent in the wil-derness, so must the Son of Man be lifted up, that whoever believes in him may have eternal life. For God so loved the world, that he gave his only Son, that whoever believes in him should not perish but have eternal life. For God did not send his Son into the world to condemn the world, but in order that the world might be saved through him. Whoever believes in him is not condemned, but whoev-

---

[14] C. H. Spurgeon, The New Park Street Pulpit, Vol. V (Pasadena, TX: Pilgrim Publications, 1981), 120.

[15] C. H. Spurgeon, *The Metropolitan Tabernacle Pulpit*, Vol. XV (Pasa-dena, TX: Pilgrim Publications, 1984), 458.

er does not believe is condemned already, because he has not believed in the name of the only Son of God.

This passage presents us with the free call of the gospel. Through the preaching of the gospel, Christ is freely offered to "whoever believes in him" (vv. 15, 16, 18). Here we have an emphasis on *human responsibility*. And we may be sure that *whoever* hears this gospel call is completely responsible to believe in Jesus for "whoever does not believe is condemned already" (v. 18).

But vv. 14–18 are seemingly in tension with vv. 19–21, which emphasize *divine sovereignty* (as well as with 3:1–8 which teaches the sovereign work of the Holy Spirit in the new birth):

> And this is the judgment: the light has come into the world, and people loved the darkness rather than the light because their works were evil. For everyone who does wicked things hates the light and does not come to the light, lest his works should be exposed. But whoever does what is true comes to the light, so that it may be clearly seen that his works have been carried out in God.

Unregenerate man does not want to depart from the sin that he loves. And left to himself he will never come into the light for fear of being shamed over the sin that he loves. How can a person who "hates the light" ever begin to love the light and freely submit to Christ unless God first changes the heart?

But notice the contrast in verse 21: "But whoever does what is true comes to the light, so that it may be clearly seen that his works have been carried out in God." The "works" spoken of here are not meritorious on the part of those doing them; otherwise, this would teach that salvation is by works. No, these works "have been carried out in God," that is, in or through union with God, and thus by His enabling power (sovereign grace).

Therefore, in John 3:14–21 we see the tension between divine sovereignty and human responsibility. Through the preaching of the gospel, Christ is freely and truly offered to "whosoever believes in Him." Those who receive the offer do so because of God's enabling grace. Those who reject the offer are totally responsible to God for their response—and they *alone* are responsible! As J. I. Packer insists:

> Whatever we may believe about election, the fact remains that a man who rejects Christ thereby becomes the cause of his own condemnation. Unbelief in the Bible is a guilty thing, and unbelievers cannot excuse themselves on the grounds that they were not elect. The unbeliever was really offered life in the gospel, and could have had it if he would; he, and no-one

> but he, is responsible for the fact that he
> rejected it, and must now endure the con-
> sequences that he rejected it.[16]

So, we are "free to respond" to the gospel. The
problem is that, in our unregenerate state, we prefer
the darkness over the light and therefore we will
never choose Christ on our own (John 3:19–20). But
the offer of the gospel is genuine, nonetheless. Man
could have Christ if only he would. And those who
reject Christ are culpable before God for the real
choice they make.

---

[16] J. I. Packer, *Evangelism and the Sovereignty of God* (Downers Grove,
IL: InterVarsity Press, 1961), 105. Packer further maintains that preachers of
the gospel have the responsibility of stressing this fact: "When we preach the
promises and invitations of the gospel, and offer Christ to sinful men and
women, it is part of our task to emphasize and re-emphasize that they are
responsible to God for the way in which they react to the good news of His
grace. No preacher can ever make this point too strongly" (Ibid., 26).

9

Does It Matter How We Live?

A question often aimed at Calvinists by non-Calvinists goes something like this: "If unconditional election is true, then does it really matter how we live?" Add to this the doctrine of *the final perseverance of the saints* and the question becomes even more pointed. This will be the topic of discussion for this chapter.

Antinomianism

The above question pertains to what theologians have long referred to as *antinomianism*, which means "against the law." It is a problem that has plagued the church since the time of the apostles. Hugh Blaire defines antinomianism as the "rejection of the moral law as a relevant part of the Christian experience."[1] In other words, it is the belief that since we as Christians have been freely justified by God's grace, it does not truly matter how we live. Kenneth Stewart captures the essence of the non-Calvinist objection when he writes:

> If any Protestants are currently suspected of this [antinomian] tendency, it is those in the Calvinist or Reformed tradition. . . . The faultfinding argument works along these lines: "If I believed in unconditional predestination as you Calvinists do, why would I not conclude that I could live however I pleased in the expectation that my decreed salvation would be unaffected?"[2]

How should Calvinists respond? First, Calvinists readily admit that there have indeed been some antinomian Calvinists through the centuries.[3]

Thankfully, however, they have been few in number. Throughout the centuries, orthodox Calvinists have consistently condemned antinomianism in their creeds, confessions, and catechisms. And rightly so, for as Orrick asserts: "The Bible teaches the eternal security of *the believer*, not the eternal security of

[1] Hugh J. Blaire, "Antinomianism" in *New International Dictionary of the Christian Church*, ed. J. D. Douglas (Grand Rapids, MI: Zondervan, 1974), 48.

[2] Stewart, *Ten Myths About Calvinism*, 156.

[3] Ibid., 151–166.

the hypocrite."[4]

Second, antinomianism is not just a Calvinist problem. The spirit of individualism is rampant in the western church today. Many professing Christians are in reality "Lone-Ranger Christians" who have little or no use for the church—much less for accountability.[5] They are an island unto themselves. They believe themselves to be in good standing with God based simply upon their belief in the doctrine of justification by faith alone. "I am not saved by works," they reason, "and grace covers all my sins. So it really doesn't matter how I live." But note carefully: Among professing Christians in western society today, *Calvinists are in the minority!* So, antinomianism is not just a Calvinist problem. In fact, I dare say that the majority of antinomians in western society today are non-Calvinists. Consequently, Stewart makes the following observation:

---

[4] Orrick, *Mere Calvinism*, 165.

[5] Horton declares: "To be sure, the Reformers emphasized the importance of personal salvation through faith in Christ. However, they would have been as baffled as the apostles with the dichotomy between 'a personal relationship with Christ' and 'belonging to the church'" (*For Calvinism*, 138). Regarding the SBC, it would appear that the vast majority of Southern Baptist "members" today are nominal Christians at best—and, I would add, *non-Calvinists* as well. Some 10,000,000 Southern Baptists are unaccounted for on a given Sunday morning. John Hammett estimates: "In 2012, average attendance at morning worship in Southern Baptist Churches was 37.6 percent of the total membership of the churches." John Hammett, "The Why and Who of Church Membership" in *Baptist Foundations: Church Government for an Anti-Institutional Age*, eds. Mark Dever and Jonathan Leeman (Nashville, TN: B&H, 2015), 168.

The Reformed theological tradition by its doctrinal confessions and catechisms, its pattern of worship (which has generally, in the past, entailed a reading of the Ten Commandments or some summary of them in connection with a corporate confession of sin), and its pulpit ministry has assuredly paid as much heed to the law of God as any expression of the Christian faith. If the Reformed theological tradition stays true to its historic bearings on this question, it may actually offer a helping hand to many beleaguered Christians in other streams of Christianity who are looking for a way out of the current antinomian malaise.[6]

Third, at least in principle, Southern Baptists have historically affirmed the need for believers to persevere in faith (or to grow in sanctification). Article IV, paragraph C on "Sanctification" of the *BF&M* reads:

Sanctification is the experience, beginning in regeneration, by which the believer is set apart to God's purposes, and is enabled to progress toward moral and spiritual maturity through the presence and power of the Holy Spirit dwelling in him. Growth in grace should continue throughout the regenerate person's life.

[6] Stewart, *Ten Myths About Calvinism*, 169.

However, I much prefer Article XII on "Sanctification" in the *Abstract of Principles* because of its stronger emphasis on the necessity of perseverance as evidence of salvation. It reads:

> Those who have been regenerated are also sanctified, by God's word and Spirit dwelling in them. This sanctification is progressive through the supply of Divine strength, *which all saints seek to obtain, pressing after a heavenly life in cordial obedience to all Christ's commands* (emphasis mine).

Baptists have likewise stressed the importance of God's preservation of the saints. Drawing heavily on the language of the *Abstract of Principles,* Article V on "God's Purpose of Grace" in the *BF&M* reads:

> *All true believers endure to the end. Those whom God has accepted in Christ, and sanctified by His Spirit, will never fall away from the state of grace, but shall persevere to the end.* Believers may fall into sin through neglect and temptation, whereby they grieve the Spirit, impair their graces and comforts, and bring reproach on the cause of Christ and temporal judgments on themselves; *yet they shall be kept by the power of God through faith unto salvation* (paragraph 2, emphasis added).

Perseverance and Preservation

Clearly, Article IV paragraph C of the BF&M affirms the *perseverance* of the saints and Article V of the BF&M affirms God's *preservation* of the saints. This is as it should be since both doctrines are taught in the Bible. We would do well to consider some examples from the New Testament.

In Philippians 1:6 Paul asserts: "And I am sure of this, that he who began a good work in you will bring it to completion at the day of Jesus Christ." That stresses God's preserving power. Then, a few verses later in Philippians 2:12–13, Paul says: "Work out your own salvation with fear and trembling, for it is God who works in you, both to will and to work for his good pleasure." That stresses both—first the believer's responsibility to persevere and then God's preserving power.

First Peter 1:5 states that ". . . by God's power [we] are being guarded through faith for a salvation ready to be revealed in the last time." That stresses God's preserving power. But then in 2 Peter 1:3–11, Peter emphasizes the believer's responsibility to persevere. Consider vv. 5–8:

> Make every effort to supplement your faith with virtue, and virtue with knowledge, and knowledge with self-control, and self-control with steadfastness, and steadfastness with godliness, and godliness with brotherly affec-

tion, and brotherly affection with love. For if
these qualities are yours and are increasing,
they keep you from being ineffective or un-
fruitful in the knowledge of our Lord Jesus
Christ.

Finally, in v. 10 Peter insists: "Be all the more dili-
gent to confirm your calling and election, for if you
practice these qualities you will never fall." Jude begins his letter in v. 1 with an emphasis on God's preserving power: "To those who are called, beloved in
God the Father and kept for Jesus Christ." Then in
vv. 20–21 Jude stresses the believer's responsibility to
persevere: "But you, beloved, building yourselves up
in your most holy faith and praying in the Holy
Spirit, keep yourselves in the love of God, waiting
for the mercy of our Lord Jesus Christ that leads to
eternal life." Jude ends the letter with another emphasis on God's preserving power as he praises Him
"who is able to keep you from stumbling and to present you blameless before the presence of his glory
with great joy" (v. 24).

To be sure, in John's Gospel the believer's responsibility to persevere is taught; but the greater emphasis is on God's preserving power. Nowhere is this
more clearly seen than in John 6:37, 39–40, 44:[7]

---

[7] Regarding John 6:37, 39–40, 44, even the Arminian scholar, I. H. Marshall, insists: "Nowhere else in the New Testament is the fact of divine
preservation of the disciples of Jesus so clearly presented as here, and no
theology of perseverance and apostasy must fail to give these verses their full

> All that the Father gives me will come to me,
> and whoever comes to me I will never cast
> out. . . . And this is the will of him who sent
> me, that I should lose nothing of all that he
> has given me, but raise it up on the last day.
> For this is the will of my Father, that every-
> one who looks on the Son and believes in him
> should have eternal life, and I will raise him
> up on the last day. . . . No one can come to
> me unless the Father who sent me draws him.
> And I will raise him up on the last day.

In John 10:27 Jesus says: "My sheep hear my voice, and I know them, and they follow me." The implication is that, if indeed we are among Jesus' sheep, we *will* persevere in the faith. Then, in John 10:28–29 Jesus proceeds to assure His disciples of God's preserving power: "I give them eternal life, and they will never perish, and no one will snatch them out of my hand. My Father, who has given them to me, is greater than all, and no one is able to snatch them out of the Father's hand." In John 15:5–6, 8–10 Jesus again stresses the believer's responsibil-ity:

> I am the vine; you are the branches. Whoever
> abides in me and I in him, he it is that bears
> much fruit, for apart from me you can do
> nothing. If anyone does not abide in me he is

value" (*Kept By the Power of God*, 181).

thrown away like a branch and withers; and
the branches are gathered, thrown into the
fire, and burned. . . . By this my Father is glorified, that you bear much fruit and so prove
to be my disciples. As the Father has loved
me, so have I loved you. Abide in my love. If
you keep my commandments, you will abide
in my love, just as I have kept my Father's
commandments and abide in his love.

Then, in John 17—a chapter featuring Christ's
Great High Priestly prayer—Jesus says in verse 2:
"While I was with them, I kept them in your name,
which you have given me. I have guarded them, and
not one of them has been lost except the son of destruction, that the Scripture might be fulfilled." And
in 17:11b Jesus prays: "Holy Father, keep them in
your name, which you have given me." This is strong
language about God's preserving power.

When we come to the book of Hebrews, we find
some of the strongest warnings against apostasy in
all the New Testament (Heb. 2:1–4; 3:12–14; 4:1–2,
11; 5:11–6:12; 10:19–39).[8] The writer often exhorts

---

[8] It is beyond the scope of this chapter to deal with the subject of apostasy
(abandoning or falling away from the faith). However, Tom Schreiner's
comments are worth noting: "A common objection [by Arminians] is that
warning passages are superfluous and beside the point if believers can't
apostatize. Such an objection, though it initially sounds plausible, reads the
biblical text as an abstraction and does not take into account that God is a
God of both means and ends. . . . God promises that all those who are justified and chosen by him will never be forsaken, that they will never totally
and finally fall away from God. Such a promise doesn't preclude the use of

his readers to persevere in the faith. At the same time, Hebrews provides us with some of the strongest teaching about Jesus' Great High Priestly ministry in all the New Testament. In 7:25 the writer asserts: "Consequently, he is able to save to the uttermost those who draw near to God through him, since he always lives to make intercession for them." Think about the implications of this. Will the prayers of Jesus Christ, our Great High Priest in heaven, ever go unanswered? Absolutely not! So, even in a book with many strong warnings about apostasy and admonitions for persevering in faith, we have this assurance that our salvation is secure because of the ongoing, intercessory prayer ministry of our Great High Priest and not on the basis of our own feeble efforts of persisting in our own faith or righteousness.

We Persevere *Because* God Preserves Us

Of course, most Southern Baptists (Calvinist or not) affirm the doctrine that is often referred to as *the eternal security of the believer* (or as some prefer to

---

means, and . . . the warnings are one of the primary means God uses to preserve his own from falling away. The end is not cast in doubt by the means that should be employed but is actually supported and undergirded by the means." Thomas R. Schreiner, *Commentary on Hebrews* in Biblical Theology for Christian Proclamation, eds. T. Desmond Alexander, Andreas J. Kostenberger and Thomas R. Schreiner (Nashville, TN: B&H Publishing Group, 2015), 489–490. Boice and Ryken avow: "These passages provoke us to higher levels of commitment and greater godliness, which is what they were given to accomplish" (*The Doctrines of Grace*, 174).

say, "once saved always saved").[9] In fact, most so-called "moderate" Calvinist Southern Baptists hold to only one out of the five points—the perseverance of the saints. I am aware of one such Southern Baptist leader to whom this applies. He refers to five-point Calvinism as "extreme Calvinism" (a term he erroneously picked up from Geisler). Apparently, his concern is that, from the extreme Calvinist point of view, our secure salvation has more to do with the preservation of God *than with us*. This is troubling, to say the least—even telling!

Indeed, as we have just demonstrated, the Bible stresses both the perseverance *and* the preservation of the saints. Both are important, and neither can be sacrificed without losing something vital for the Christian life. However, if I am going to err in this matter, then you had better believe that I am going

---

[9] Consider the inconsistency of the non-Calvinist (or "Traditionalist" as some prefer) Southern Baptist position. On the one hand, they believe in libertarian freedom; yet, on the other hand, they believe in the eternal security of the believer. According to non-Calvinists, true freedom exists only when one is able to choose between two options from a posture of neutrality and without any bias. In other words, true freedom means that a person is able either to choose Christ or reject Christ. But if that is true, then once a person becomes a Christian he no longer has true freedom. Because if it is true that his salvation is eternally secure, then the possibility of choosing to reject Christ has been eliminated, and thus true freedom no longer exists. Ascol explains it this way: "If the nature of fallen man's will is such that he has the power of contrary choice either to trust Christ or reject Christ, how and why is this power lost once such a man becomes a Christian? Why must a Christian always remain a Christian? How can God keep him in the faith without 'vitiating' his free will? It seems like this scheme leaves Christians with less of an 'actual free will' . . . after conversion than before" (*Traditional Theology & the SBC*, 82).

to err more so on the side of God's preserving power than on our ability to persevere! Because if my salvation has more to do with *my* perseverance than *God's* preservation, then I am on shaky ground and my salvation is not very secure after all.

In Luke 22:31–32 Jesus says to Peter: "Simon, Simon, behold, Satan demanded to have you, that he might sift you like wheat, but I have prayed for you that your faith may not fail. And when you have turned again, strengthen your brothers." Peterson is surely right when he asserts: "Why did [Peter] succeed? Not because of the greatness of his dedication to Christ. He persevered because his Lord preserved him by praying for him."[10] And so it is with all of Jesus' sheep! Though we as believers may stumble and fall, we will not ultimately be lost (John 6:39). Indeed, God assures us in His Word that He will preserve unto the end every single one of His own.

Of course, that does not mean we may presume upon God's grace. We are responsible to persevere in the faith. God will *preserve* His own, but He will not do it apart from our *perseverance*. That is the tension we find in Scripture. And yet, we must admit that even our perseverance is the Father's gift. We

[10] Robert A. Peterson, *Our Secure Salvation: Preservation and Apostasy* in Explorations of Biblical Theology series, ed. Robert A. Peterson (Phillipsburg, NJ: P&R Publishing, 2009), 47. Leon Morris avows: "It is one of the precious things about the Christian faith that our continuance in eternal life depends not on our feeble hold on Christ, but on His firm grip on us." Leon Morris, *The Gospel According to John*, The New International Commentary on the New Testament (Grand Rapids, MI: Eerdmans, 1971), 521.

persevere because God preserves us! No one in heaven will be claiming: "I made it because of my own grit and determination to persevere in faith!" No, from beginning to end it is *all* of God, and God will get *all* of the glory for it (1 Cor. 1:30–31, 4:7; Gal. 6:14; Phil. 3:3; Rev. 19:1).

Not Arrogance or Antinomianism, But Humility and Holiness

Rather than leading to arrogance and/or antinomianism, these two doctrines—*unconditional election* and *the perseverance/preservation of the saints*—should lead to deep humility and a hunger for holiness. Consequently, regarding the doctrine of election, the *BF&M* states: "It excludes boasting and promotes humility." Moreover, in Ephesians 1:4 Paul says: "He chose us in him before the foundation of the world, that we should be holy and blameless before him." Then, in Ephesians 2:10 Paul writes: "For we are his workmanship, created in Christ Jesus for good works, which God prepared beforehand, that we should walk in them."

Finally, consider Selph's remarks about Paul's teaching in Romans:

> *In view of God's mercies* (Romans 12:1), Paul said, reflecting upon *God's electing mercy* from Romans 8–11, "you should give your bodies and minds (12:1, 2) to serve God in the

church (12:3–8), in loving brethren and enemies (12:9–21), in obeying the government (13:1–7), in living a life of godly love (13:8–14), and in practicing self-denying Christian liberty (Chapter 14, 15)." What the Holy Spirit is really saying through the Apostle Paul is this—You must understand God's electing purpose and electing mercies before you will be able to live the daily Christian life of holiness and good works in the way our God desires. Every action and reaction in the Christian's life is to flow from a sanctified heart and mind that has been shaped by the grace of Unconditional Election.[11]

Over and again we see this pattern in Paul's writings, as well as in other New Testament letters. So, yes, it does matter how we live. It matters because God, our Creator, says without qualification or ambiguity that it matters. Antinomianism is contrary to true Calvinism; it is contrary to the teaching of Scripture. As Selph declares: "No one has any Biblical right to lay claim to be God's elect or His child if holiness of daily life is not top priority."[12] Indeed, "without holiness no man shall see the Lord" (Heb. 12:14).

[11] Selph, *Southern Baptists and the Doctrine of Election*, 155–156.
[12] Ibid., 153. The quote by Orrick on pp. 114–115 bears repeating: "The Bible teaches the eternal security of *the believer*, not the eternal security of the hypocrite" (*Mere Calvinism*, 165).

IO

Does Calvinism Discourage Evangelism?

Does Calvinism discourage evangelism? Absolutely not! Just the opposite is true, as this chapter will reveal. But unfortunately, this is yet another caricature often made about Calvinism by non-Calvinists. I can think of at least three reasons why I believe this is so.

(1) *Non-Calvinists confuse Calvinism with hyper-Calvinism.* Hyper-Calvinism minimizes, or outright denies, genuine human responsibility, downplays the importance of prayer, and frowns on evangelism and missions. Calvinism, however, affirms all of this and more! Iain Murray draws the following distinctions:

> Arminians say that sinners are commanded [to repent and believe the gospel], therefore they must be able; hyper-Calvinists say they are not able, therefore they cannot be com-

manded. But Scripture and Calvinism sets forth *both* man's inability and his duty, and both truths are a necessary part of evangelism—the former reveals the sinner's need of a help which only God can give, and the latter, which is expressed in the exhortations, promises and invitations of Scripture, shows him the place in which his peace and safety lies, namely, the person of the Son of God.[1]

To be sure, when it comes to evangelism, there is a ditch on both sides, and we must be careful to avoid them. As Timothy George warns:

It is possible to get out of theological balance by overemphasizing either the human role in conversion or the divine initiative in salvation. Arminians have sometimes been guilty of the former. Their theology obscures the real meaning of grace and reduces God to a puppet on a string. Hyper-Calvinists have frequently fallen into the opposite error, so exalting God's sovereignty that human responsibility and free moral agency are denied.

[1] Iain H. Murray, *The Forgotten Spurgeon*, Reset Edition (Carlisle, PA: The Banner of Truth Trust, 2009), 106. Murray further notes: "Hyper-Calvinism in its attempt to square all gospel truth with God's purpose to save the elect, denies there is a universal command to repent and believe, and asserts that we have only warrant to invite to Christ those who are *conscious* of a sense of sin and need. In other words, it is those who have been spiritually quickened to seek a Savior and not those who are in the death of unbelief and indifference, to whom the exhortations of the gospel must be addressed" (Ibid., 49).

> *Christians must ever be on guard against both extremes!* Either one is deadly to the purpose of evangelism and missions.[2]

(2) *Non-Calvinists assume that evangelism must be a futile exercise.* I have literally had people say to me: "If God already has His team picked out, then what's the point of evangelism? *Que sera sera*— Whatever will be, will be!"[3] In 1997 the Baptist historian William Estep spoke for many non-Calvinists when he referred to Calvinism as "logically anti-

---

[2] George, *Amazing Grace*, 103.

[3] Many non-Calvinists mistakenly equate *fatalism* with predestination. But as Adam Murrell explains: "Fatalism can best be summed up with the words *que sera sera*, whatever will be, will be. The biblical doctrine of predestination, however, upholds that God from all eternity had one immutable plan for His creation. His decrees will never falter nor are they irrational or impersonal. All things work together for good for those who love God (Rom 8:28). Only predestination maintains the belief in a final cause, an idea that God has control over the outcome of all events. Nothing, therefore, is left to chance. Everything that comes to pass is part of a greater paradigm, one that cannot be fully understood by finite creatures because of our limitations. . . . The biblical perspective is that the world and all of its inhabitants were decreed before time began by an all-knowing, all-powerful, and all-loving God" Adam Murrell, *Predestined to Believe: Common Objections to the Reformed Faith Answered*, Second Edition (Eugene, OR: Resource Publications, 2009), 70. Sproul affirms: "Fatalism literally means that the affairs of men are controlled either by whimsical sub-deities (the Fates) or more popularly by impersonal forces of chance. Predestination is based neither on a mythical view of goddesses playing with our lives nor upon a view of destiny controlled by the chance collision of atoms. Predestination is rooted in the character of a personal and righteous God, a God who is the sovereign Lord of history" (*Chosen By God*), 191. On a similar note, many non-Calvinists equate the Calvinist's view of God's sovereign choice with *arbitrariness*. But according to Selph: "Sovereignty is to be distinguished from arbitrariness. In the latter, the will of the agent directs the actions, without references to a wise and good pleasure. [God's] pleasure is good, because it is always directed to his own perfections" (*Southern Baptists and the Doctrine of Election*, 49).

missionary."[4] But the Calvinist does not see it this way at all. As J. I. Packer declares:

> So far from making evangelism pointless, the sovereignty of God in grace is the one thing that prevents evangelism from being pointless. . . . Were it not for the sovereign grace of God, evangelism would be the most futile and useless enterprise that the world has ever seen, and there would be no more complete waste of time under the sun than to preach the Christian gospel.[5]

Consider the following four truths about evangelism and missions:

First, God commands us to do evangelism and missions. J. I. Packer speaks for Calvinism when he claims: "We . . . have a responsibility for making the gospel known. . . . Evangelism is the inalienable responsibility of every Christian community, and every Christian man."[6] Enough said.

Second, God works through means. According to Romans 10:13–15, no one will be saved without calling on the name of the Lord. And no one will call

---

[4] William Estep, "Calvinizing Southern Baptists" in *Texas Baptist Standard*, March 26, 1997.

[5] Packer, *Evangelism and the Sovereignty of God*, 106.

[6] Ibid., 26. Sproul insists: "Evangelism is our duty. God has commanded it. That should be enough to end the matter. But there is more. Evangelism is not only a duty; it is also a privilege. God allows us to participate in the greatest work in human history, the work of redemption" (*Chosen By God*), 209.

upon His name unless they first hear the gospel. And no one will hear the gospel unless someone goes and proclaims it to them. This is the divine process. The gospel is the means through which God saves the elect. As Adam Murrell observes:

> God could have chosen any means He wanted in order to bring His people salvation, but for reasons unbeknownst to us, He has chosen the folly of preaching to bring about salvation. He could have personally whispered in people's ears, or He could have visited some in dreams or visions, but He chose not to do so. He has decreed the preaching of the Word unto salvation.[7]

Third, God's sovereignty in salvation actually stimulates evangelism and missions. For example, when Spurgeon was asked why he preached if only some are elected for salvation, he replied:

> That is why we preach! If there are so many fish to be taken in the net, I will go and catch some of them. Because many are ordained to be caught, I spread my nets with eager expectation. I never could see why that should repress our zealous efforts. It seems to me to be the very thing that should awaken us with energy—that God has a people, and that these

[7] Murrell, *Predestined to Believe*, 77.

131

people shall be brought in.[8]

Rather than discouraging evangelism, God's sovereignty in salvation assured Paul of the success of evangelism (Acts 13:48). It motivated him to "endure everything for the sake of the elect, that they also may obtain the salvation that is in Christ Jesus with eternal glory" (2 Tim. 2:10). Regarding Romans 10:1 Selph observes: "The same God who comforted Paul with the assurance of success in view of the conquering purpose of election (chapters 9 and 11), also ignited within Paul's soul a consuming desire to reach as many men as God would allow him to reach."[9]

Fourth, zeal for God's name to be honored among the nations is the primary motivation for missions. In Romans 1:5 Paul speaks of his assignment to "bring about the obedience of faith for the sake of his name among all the nations." Regarding this verse, John Stott comments:

> We should be "jealous" (as Scripture sometimes puts it) for the honour of his name—troubled when it remains unknown, hurt when it is ignored, indignant when it is blas-

[8] Quoted in Peterson, *Election and Free Will*, 177. Charles Haddon Spurgeon, *Metropolitan Tabernacle Pulpit*, Vol. XVI (Pasadena, TX: Pilgrim Publications, 1981), 622.

[9] Selph, *Southern Baptists and the Doctrine of Election*, 145. About this, Orrick writes: "This . . . frees me from despair when I do not see the results I might wish. Preaching is my work. Evangelizing is my work. Praying is my work. Salvation is God's work. The one who planned in eternity past to redeem a people for himself will see the job finished" (*Mere Calvinism*, 76).

phemed, and all the time anxious and deter-
mined that it shall be given the honour and
glory which are due to it. The highest of missionary motives is neither obedience to the
Great Commission (important as that is), nor
love for sinners who are alienated and perishing (strong as the incentive is, especially when
we contemplate the wrath of God . . .), but
rather zeal—burning and passionate zeal—
for the glory of Jesus Christ.[10]

According to Piper, zeal for God's name to be honored among the nations so that more and more people can know and worship our God is the primary
motivation for missions. In other words, God's goal
is for His chosen people to worship Him forever and
missions is the means through which this goal is to
be accomplished.[11]

(3) *Non-Calvinists are ignorant about Calvinist
missions history.* The truth is that some of the most
zealous missionaries in history have been Calvinists.
Selph writes:

[10] John R. W. Stott, *Romans: God's Good News for the World* (Downers
Grove, IL: InterVarsity, 1994), 53.

[11] Piper declares: "Missions is not the ultimate goal of the church. Worship is. Missions exists because worship doesn't. Worship is ultimate, not
missions, because God is ultimate, not man. When this age is over, and
countless millions of the redeemed fall on their faces before the throne of
God, missions will be no more. It is a temporary necessity. But worship
abides forever." John Piper, *Let the Nations Be Glad! The Supremacy of
God in Missions*, Third Edition (Grand Rapids, MI: Baker Academic, 2010),
15.

Consider all the major missionary move-
ments, along with the Great Awakenings in
America. Consider the great Protestant Reformation in Europe. It is easily demonstrated
that believers in Unconditional Election have
led the way in missionary zeal and effort.
Spurgeon loved to speak to this topic: "The
greatest missionaries that have ever lived have
believed in God's choice of them; and instead
of this doctrine leading to inaction, it has ever
been an irresistible motive power, and it will
be again."[12]

A Long Line of Calvinist Missions

On his blog, Kevin DeYoung provides a sampling of
historically notable Calvinists who have greatly in-
fluenced foreign missions. There, we find this im-
pressive listing:

John Calvin: Calvin sent missionaries from
Geneva into France and as far away as Brazil.
Most of these young men sent to France died
a martyr's death, but the church of Geneva
continued to send them.[13]

[12] Selph, *Southern Baptists and the Doctrine of Election*, 142. Quote by
Spurgeon cited in Murray, *The Forgotten Spurgeon*, 100–101.

[13] Many people are surprised to learn that John Calvin himself was very
missions-minded. In a sermon on 1 Timothy 2:3–5 Calvin said: "Thus we
may see what St. Paul's meaning is when he saith, God will have His grace
made known to all the world, and His gospel preached to all creatures.
Therefore, we must endeavor, as much as possible, to persuade those who
are strangers to the faith, and seem to be utterly deprived of the goodness of

John Eliot: A missionary sent to the American Indians in the 1600s. He is believed to be the first missionary among this people group. As many have said, if William Carey is the father of the modern mission's movement, then John Eliot is its grandfather.

David Brainerd: A missionary to the American Indians in the 1700s. Many historians believe that he has sent more individuals into the mission field than any other person in the history of the church via his diary, *An Account of the Life of the Late Reverend David Brainerd*.

Theodorus Frelinghuysen: The great evangelist and preacher, who set the stage for the First Great Awakening in the middle colonies.

Jonathan Edwards: The great theologian, writer, and preacher of the First Great Awakening. He was also a missionary to the Indians.

George Whitfield: The great voice and preacher of the First Great Awakening. He journeyed across the Atlantic Ocean thirteen times and scholars believe he preached over 18,000 sermons.

William Tennent: He founded the Log College, which later became Princeton University. This college trained pastors and pro-

God, to accept salvation. Jesus Christ is not only a Savior of a few, but He offereth Himself to all." John Calvin, "Sermon on 1 Tim. 2:3–5" in *Calvin's Sermons: The Mystery of Godliness* (Grand Rapids, MI: Eerdmans, 1950).

vided many of the revivalist preachers of the First Great Awakening.

Samuel Davies: The famous President of the College of New Jersey (Princeton University), preacher of the First Great Awakening, and evangelist to the slaves of Virginia. It is believed that hundreds of slaves came to saving faith through his evangelism efforts.

William Carey: He is the famous missionary to India and is considered the father of the modern mission's movement.

Robert Moffat: The first missionary to reach the interior of Africa with the Gospel. He translated the entire Bible and Pilgrim's Progress into Setswana.

David Livingstone: Arguably, the most famous missionary to the continent of Africa.

Robert Morrison: The first Protestant missionary to China and the first to translate the Bible into Chinese.

Peter Parker: An American physician and missionary to China who first introduced Western medical techniques to the Chinese. He also served as the president of the Medical Missionary Society of China.

Adoniram Judson: The famous missionary to Burma, translated the Bible into Burmese, and established multiple Baptist Churches in Burma. His mission work led many to enter the mission field and was foundational for forming the first Baptist association in America.[14]

Charles Simeon: The vicar of Holy Trinity Church and the founding figure of the Church Missionary Society. This organization was instrumental in leading many students to the mission field. The Society itself has sent more than 9,000 missionaries into the world.

Henry Martyn: The renowned missionary to India and Persia. He preached in the face of opposition and translated the New Testament into a number of languages.

Samuel Zwemer: He is affectionately known as "The Apostle to Islam." His legacy includes efforts in Bahrain, Arabia, Egypt, and Asia Minor. His writing was used by the Lord to encourage and mobilize an entire generation of missionaries to labor in Islamic countries.

John Stott: Scholar, ... pastor, and evangelist of the twentieth century. He was one of the principle authors and the influential leader in establishing the Lausanne Covenant, which promoted world-wide evangelism.

Francis Schaeffer: Pastor and founder of L'Abri, which has been used by the Lord to

---

[14] According to Ascol: "Through [Judson's] labors and those of Luther Rice, The Triennial Convention was established in 1814 for the purpose of supporting the work of Judson in Burma. This body was the precursor to the Southern Baptist Convention that marks its beginning in 1845" (*Traditional Theology & the SBC*, 85).

draw many to saving faith as they intellectually wrestled with the tenants of Christianity.

D. James Kennedy: The founder of Evangelism Explosion, which many believe is the most widely used evangelistic training curriculum in church history.

John Piper: Pastor, writer, and theologian, who has been used by the Lord to define missions and send many young people into the mission field.[15]

Indeed, many others could have made the list, including the famed English Baptist pastor, C. H. Spurgeon and the early American Baptist, Luther Rice, to mention just two.[16]

A Rich Calvinistic Heritage of SBC Missions

Furthermore, many of our SBC missionaries today are Calvinists. But this has been the case ever since the very founding of the SBC. Of course, this will come as no surprise to those who know their SBC missions history. As Ascol observes: "The SBC was organized to serve churches specifically by 'eliciting, combining, and directing the energies of the denomi-

[15] Kevin DeYoung, *Does Calvinism Kill Missions?*, The Gospel Coalition, July 3, 2013; available at https://www.thegospelcoalition.org/blogs/kevin-deyoung/does-calvinism-kill-missions/.

[16] Readers are strongly encouraged to listen to David Platt's message titled "Divine Sovereignty: The Fuel of Death-Defying Missions" (Session VI), Together For The Gospel, 2012; available at https://t4g.org/media/2012/05/divine-sovereignty-the-fuel-of-death-defying-missions-2/.

nation for the propagation of the gospel'."[17] Non-Calvinist Southern Baptists who believe that Calvinism discourages missions would do well to reflect upon the following remarks by Selph:

> It is often claimed that the preaching of doctrine and certainly the doctrine of Unconditional Election, will sap the church of evangelistic zeal and drive. . . . If their claims be true, one searching question must be asked—What happened in the Southern Baptist Convention for [the first] eighty years? . . . Unconditional Election was the foundation of all doctrinal views that ignited the convention to be the greatest evangelistic and missionary force that it was. How did it happen? How did the [so-called] "hyper-Calvinists" ever get untracked and have any evangelistic concern if these claims be true?[18]

Conclusion

Calvinism in no way can be said to discourage evangelism, even in the least little bit! Consequently, to claim, as one Southern Baptist Associational Missionary does, that five-point Calvinists are "extreme" because they place little or no emphasis on evangelism and missions is outrageous given the historical

---

[17] Ascol, *Traditional Theology & the SBC*, 85.
[18] Selph, *Southern Baptists and the Doctrine of Election*, 142.

evidence.[19] One has to be either ignorant of Calvinist missions history or downright spiteful to make such an unfounded assertion. It is one thing to disagree with Calvinists about the doctrines of grace; it is quite another thing altogether to accuse five-point Calvinists of placing little or no emphasis on evangelism and missions. It may seem illogical to non-Calvinists that someone can believe in unconditional election and be evangelistic and missions-minded at the same time. But history proves that many have done just that! Consequently, Stewart is surely right to assert: "Alarmist statements, made in these last decades in the face of the current resurgence of interest in Reformed theology, surely ought to give way to more careful assessments if missions history is to be trusted."[20]

---

[19] I wholeheartedly agree with Orrick, who contends: "In the face of such ample historical evidence, I am sometimes shocked to hear men who ought to know better make the unfounded assertion that Calvinism kills missions and evangelism. It might kill unbiblical, manipulative evangelistic methodologies, but it does not kill missions and evangelism" (*Mere Calvinism*, 21).

[20] Stewart, *Ten Myths About Calvinism*, 147.

II

Final Appeals

It is fitting to conclude this book with some final appeals. I have five specific groups in mind.

(1) *To non-Calvinists who are wrestling with the doctrines of grace: Stay in the Word!*

Prior to my becoming a Calvinist, I remember that I would often bump up against the doctrines of grace in the Scriptures to the point of almost embracing them. As I went on my way, however, my mind and emotions resisted them with all the energy they could muster. But then every time I would return to the Scriptures, I would again be confronted repeatedly with these doctrines. It was only a matter of time before I saw them everywhere in the Bible. My simple testimony is that Scripture won out. Yes, I was one of those "reluctant converts." But then to my delight, I very quickly grew to love the doctrines of grace—once I understood the implications of what they actually taught. After I understood how they exposed God's grace and mercy, while simultaneously maintaining His sovereignty and prerogatives, they became sweet to my soul. And I later learned that many people down through the centuries have had a similar experience. But my point in relating this experience is to appeal to you to *stay in the Word!* Ultimately, what matters is not what "makes sense" to our finite minds or what "feels right" in our hearts. Rather, at the end of the day, all that really matters is what the Word of God teaches. So, stay in the Word!

(2) *To non-Calvinists who adamantly oppose the doctrines of grace: Don't misrepresent Calvinism!*

Some non-Calvinists are cordial toward their Calvinistic brothers and sisters in Christ. Others harbor a deep-seated animosity toward the doctrines of grace and would love to see Calvinism eradicated from the planet. Most probably land somewhere in between, tolerant of Calvinism but hoping its influence diminishes. Regardless of where you may fall personally, my appeal is the same: *Don't misrepresent Calvinism!* Unfortunately, much of the information about Calvinism being dispensed by non-Calvinists within the SBC today is grossly misleading. Of all people, Christian leaders should take the greatest care to articulate theology as accurately as possible—even that of their opponents. Concern for truth and close attention to accuracy is imperative, or legitimate critique that may be warranted will carry no weight. The two camps (Calvinists and non-Calvinists) will not make progress towards a more harmonious relationship in the SBC by misrepresenting one another. So please, get your facts straight and don't misrepresent Calvinism!

(3) *To Calvinists who unashamedly embrace the doctrines of grace: Be gracious!*

The fact that Calvinists are so often misrepresented by non-Calvinists can be very frustrating, to say the least. But if we are not careful, in our zeal to defend the truth we Calvinists can easily cross over into self-righteous pride and anger unawares. I confess that I have not always handled my anger properly and I humbly repent for the times I have failed in this regard. I do not want to be known as one of those angry Calvinists that Pastor Joe Thorn spoke about (see p. 21). I do not want you to be one either. So I appeal to all my Calvinist friends: Be zealous. Be bold. Be unashamed of the gospel. But be gracious! We cannot build bridges with our non-Calvinist Southern Baptist brothers and sisters any other way.

Furthermore, in your handling of the doctrines of grace, be discreet! As Orrick advises:

> Be wise. Not everything that needs to be said needs to be said right now. With the knowledge of these doctrines comes the responsibility to be a wise soul physician. Most

medicine is to be administered gradually and over time. These doctrines are offensive enough to the natural man without making them more offensive through pushy, belligerent arguments. The medicine is already bitter; it is even harder to swallow when it is boiling hot. Discretion is not deception, nor is it cowardice. Jesus recognized that his disciples were not ready to receive everything that they needed to know. "I still have many things to say to you, but you cannot bear them now" (John 16:12). So he waited for the Holy Spirit to reveal these things to them later. If the Lord Jesus could patiently wait for the Holy Spirit to reveal truth, surely you and I can as well.[1]

This is excellent advice! However, there is a flip side to this coin, so it needs to be taken along with the advice offered under the next heading.

(4) *To Calvinists who are timid regarding the doctrines of grace: Be courageous!*

From time to time, I encounter Calvinists who are brave around other Calvinists but, for whatever reason, are timid outside of those circles. Perhaps it is because of the stigma attached to the label in certain SBC circles today. Believe me, I know. Being ostracized in the SBC for being a Calvinist is indeed a sad irony given our Southern Baptist heritage. But such

[1] Orrick, *Mere Calvinism* , 78–79.

are the times in which we are living. Perhaps some are timid due to the cost involved. Being a Calvinist today can cost you relationships, reputation, or even your job (or a prospective job). Believe me, I know about that too. But this is no time to be a "closet Calvinist," Tom Ascol admonishes:

> One of the greatest challenges that faces every pastor is the courage to stay true to his convictions. This is especially true when those convictions, though deeply and clearly rooted in Scripture, are out of step with popular opinion or the prevailing desires of influential church members. . . . Even more common is the subtle pressure that pastors often feel to compromise their convictions for the sake of peace. . . . The gospel that has been secured for us and entrusted to us at . . . great cost is worthy of . . . courage on the part of those who are stewards of it.[2]

So I appeal to you my timid Calvinist friends: Be humble. Be gentle. Be gracious. But *be courageous!*[3]

---

[2] From an online article, "Charles Spurgeon and Courage in the Pulpit" (Founders Ministries, March 16, 2017); available at https://founders.org/2017/03/16/charles-spurgeon-and-courage-in-the-pulpit/.

[3] George declares: "We are not free to ignore the doctrine of predestination simply because we do not like it, cannot understand it, or do not see how it can be squared with a particular philosophical understanding of reality. If we affirm the verbal inspiration of the Bible, as we should, then we know that God has wasted no words in revealing his will to us. There are many doctrinal truths we may not be able to understand perfectly in this life, but God has revealed them to us for a purpose. It is our duty to rightly

(5) To non-Christians who are searching for truth: Come to Jesus!

Perhaps some of my readers are not professing Christians. If so, I want to thank you for taking the time to read this book. But how truly sad it would be for me to write an entire book about the doctrines of grace—even stressing at certain points how important it is that preachers make an appeal for sinners to come to Christ—and then fail to do so myself. So, I appeal to you, my non-Christian friends: *Come to Jesus!* Do not be put off or distracted by the finer points of theology that we Calvinists and non-Calvinists have been debating for centuries. Do not concern yourself with whether or not you are among the elect. You do not need to ask: "Am I one of the elect or not?" No, the question of the hour is this: "What must I do to be saved?" I urge you to heed the following counsel of J. I. Packer:

> To the question: what must I do to be saved? The old gospel replies: believe on the Lord Jesus Christ. To the question: what does it mean to believe on the Lord Jesus Christ? its reply is: it means knowing oneself to be a sinner, and Christ to have died for sinners; abandoning all self-righteousness and self-confidence, and casting oneself wholly upon

divide the Word of truth so that we may understand it more fully and thus love and serve God more faithfully until in heaven we shall see 'face to face' (1 Cor. 13:12) [*Amazing Grace*, 129].

Him for pardon and peace; and exchanging one's natural enmity and rebellion against God for a spirit of grateful submission to the will of Christ through the renewing of one's heart by the Holy Spirit. And to the further question still: how am I to go about believing on Christ and repenting, if I have no natural ability to do these things? It answers: look to Christ, speak to Christ, cry to Christ, just as you are; confess your sin, your impenitence, your unbelief, and cast yourself on His mercy; ask Him to give you a new heart, working in you true repentance and firm faith; ask Him to take away your evil heart of unbelief and to write His law within you, that you may never henceforth stray from Him. Turn to Him and trust Him as best you can, and pray for grace to turn and trust more thoroughly; use the means of grace expectantly, looking to Christ to draw near to you as you seek to draw near to Him; watch, pray, read, and hear God's Word, worship and commune with God's people, and so continue til you know in yourself beyond doubt that you are indeed a changed being, a penitent believer, and the new heart which you desired has been put in you.[4]

[4] J. I. Packer, *The Quest for Godliness* (Wheaton, IL: Crossway, 1994), 144.

I close with the encouraging words of our Lord and Savior, Jesus Christ, who said: "Come to me, all who labor and are heavy laden, and I will give you rest. Take my yoke upon you, and learn from me, for I am gentle and lowly in heart, and you will find rest for your souls. For my yoke is easy, and my burden is light" (Matt. 11:28–30).

APPENDIX I

Altar Calls

A common concern among many non-Calvinist Southern Baptists is that Calvinist preachers tend to shy away from giving altar calls. For some non-Calvinists, this is ample evidence that Calvinists place little or no emphasis on evangelism. But nothing could be further from the truth. For the vast majority of Southern Baptists, the altar call is a long-cherished tradition. Consequently, most have never once questioned the practice. But we would do well to reflect upon a few important truths regarding this matter.

A Brief History of the Altar Call

Many Southern Baptists today are unaware of the history of the altar call.[1] The practice originated dur-

[1] See article by Thomas Kidd, "A Brief History of the Altar Call" (The

ing the revivals of the early nineteenth century. That means it has only been around for roughly two hundred years. Think about that for just a moment. Baptists have been around for a little over four hundred years now! Selph observes:

> The Christian Church knew nothing of an altar call for over 1800 years. Surprisingly enough, people were converted without them for many years, and the church did just fine. This, of course, is an understatement. The Gospel under the Spirit's power was sufficient to transform lives through the ages without the church having to adopt extra-Biblical measures.[2]

Most historians point to the Arminian revivalist Charles G. Finney as the innovator. Iain Murray writes: "C. G. Finney (1792–1875), apparently the first evangelist to call people forward during a service to a position which he called 'the anxious seat,' defended the practice on the grounds that it answered the purpose which baptism had in the days of the apostles."[3] Unbelievable! But as Selph rightly argues: "The public profession of faith is done at baptism. . . . *Baptism* is God's appointed means to pub-

Gospel Coalition, July 24, 2017); available at https://www.thegospelcoalition.org/blogs/evangelical-history/a-brief-history-of-the-altar-call/.

[2] Selph, *Southern Baptists and the Doctrine of Election*, 131.

[3] Iain H. Murray, *The Invitation System* (Carlisle, PA: The Banner of Truth Trust, 2002), 10.

licly confess the Lord, not an altar call."[4] Indeed, this is exactly what we find in the pages of the New Testament!

Finally, consider the fact that three of the most successful evangelists in church history—George Whitfield, Jonathan Edwards, and John Wesley—never gave an altar call! Instead, they made the appeal for sinners to come to Christ in their sermons and often counseled them afterwards, leaving the results with God.[5] This leads right into the next point for consideration.

Confusion About the Altar Call

Many confuse a public appeal for decision with the altar call.[6] On the one hand, gospel preachers should boldly and passionately invite sinners to "come to Jesus" and to "put their trust in Jesus." Selph insists: "The good news is to be heartily and boldly set forth. The warnings and promises, the duties and blessings . . . and all the appropriate applications of the gospel are to be declared with a burning passion and a holy urgency."[7] On the other hand, we should not confuse a public appeal with the altar call. For as Selph further states: "The gospel is no less pro-

[4] Selph, *Southern Baptists and the Doctrine of Election*, 132.
[5] David Bennett, *The Altar Call: Its Origins and Present Usage* (Lanham, MD: University Press of America, 2000), 21–22.
[6] See article by Nathan Rose, "On Altar Calls and Invitations" (North American Missions Board, SBC, Replant Blog, 2018) available at https://www.namb.net/replant-blog/on-altar-calls-and-invitations/.
[7] Selph, *Southern Baptists and the Doctrine of Election*, 132.

claimed without an altar call."[8]

In short, a public appeal is biblical and therefore *necessary* for faithful gospel proclamation. The altar call, however, lacks biblical support and therefore is *unnecessary* for faithful gospel proclamation. As Nettles attests:

> One should never speak against invitations, for they arise out of the necessities of New Testament faith. The gospel message itself consists of an invitation to all sinners to find forgiveness, to all the weary to find rest, and to all heavy-laden to find relief. Those who want to learn from Christ are urged to come to Him. Thus, the whole message either implies or consists of invitation—yea, even beyond invitation unto command. The reality of this, however, should not be confused with public altar calls, or . . . the invitation system. The invitation system prompts many pastors to focus on smooth methodology rather than faithful gospelizing. Unobtrusive transitions from sermon to invitation, mood, warmth, and music usurp the place of the gospel. Although characterized as evangelistic, such approaches do not deserve the distinction of the name.[9]

[8] Ibid.
[9] Nettles, *By His Grace and for His Glory*, 449–450.

Inherent Dangers in Having an Altar Call

The fact is there are *no* scriptural commands, or precedent, for altar calls. But there *are* plenty of dangers in having them—primarily that of relying more on our technique and the securing of converts than on the sovereign God who alone can save. Packer offers some keen insights on the matter:

> It is right to recognize our responsibility to engage in aggressive evangelism. It is right to desire the conversion of unbelievers. . . . But it is not right when we take it on us to do more than God has given us to do. It is not right when we regard ourselves as responsible for securing converts, and look to our own enterprise and techniques to accomplish what only God can accomplish. To do that is to intrude ourselves into the office of the Holy Ghost, and to exalt ourselves as the agents of the new birth. And the point that we must see is this: *only by letting our knowledge of God's sovereignty control the way in which we plan, and pray, and work in His service, can we avoid becoming guilty of this fault.* For where we are not consciously relying on God, there we shall inevitably be found relying on ourselves. And the spirit of self-reliance is a blight on evangelism. Such, however, is the inevitable consequence of forgetting God's sovereignty

in the conversion of souls.[10]

Moreover, during a Q&A session at a minister's conference in the 1970s, D. Martyn Lloyd-Jones was asked if Scripture justified the use of altar calls. Lloyd-Jones replied:

> I feel that this pressure which is put upon people to come forward in decision ultimately is due to a lack of faith in the work and operation of the Holy Spirit. We are to preach the Word, and if we do it properly, there will be a call to a decision that comes in the message, and then we leave it to the Spirit to act upon people. And of course He does. Some may come immediately at the close of the service to see the minister. I think there should always be an indication that the minister will be glad to see anybody who wants to put questions to him or wants further help. But that is a very different thing from putting pressure upon people to come forward. I feel it is wrong to put pressure directly on the will. The order in Scripture seems to be this—the truth is presented to the mind, which moves the heart, and that in turn moves the will.[11]

---

[10] Packer, *Evangelism and the Sovereignty of God*, 28–29.

[11] Online article, "Dr. Lloyd-Jones on the Altar Call" (Banner of Truth, June 21, 2003); available at https://banneroftruth.org/us/resources/articles/2003/dr-lloyd-jones-on-the-altar-call/.

Conclusion

Nevertheless, being unaware of their origin and having never reflected upon their inherent dangers, most SBC congregations today expect their pastor to give altar calls. And the newly called pastor will be wise to do so—even if he is uncomfortable with the practice. Otherwise, he will be accused of placing little or no emphasis on evangelism—even if that is not the case. So it would probably be wise in such a context to honor the cherished tradition so as not to cause unnecessary offense. But more importantly, pastors must honor the Lord by refusing to "intrude ourselves into the office of the Holy Ghost." How can this be accomplished? At the risk of oversimplification, I strongly suggest the following approach: (1) Present the gospel and make an appeal for a decision *in your sermon*. (2) When the invitation is given, avoid any and every manner of manipulative methodologies. In other words, get out of the way and let the Spirit do the convicting.[12]

[12] For more information on the inherent dangers of altar calls see Jonathan Leeman, "You Asked: Should Churches Perform Altar Calls?" (The Gospel Coalition, November 16, 2011); available at https://www.thegospel coalition.org/article/you-asked-should-churches-perform-altar-calls/.

Elder-Led Polity[1]

The assertion is sometimes made by non-Calvinists that what typically goes hand-in-hand with historic Calvinism is a shift from being a congregational decision making body to an elder-led polity. This is problematic for at least two reasons.

(1) *There is no empirical proof substantiating this assertion.* Indeed, there are many Southern Baptist churches today that affirm the doctrines of grace but do not have an elder-led polity. A plurality of elders is not an essential mark of a true church, anyway. In other words, a church can be a true church with or without an elder-led polity.[2] Furthermore, there are a

---

[1] The discussion here has been adapted from Appendix A: "Elder-Led Congregationalism" of my doctoral dissertation, *A Well-Ordered Hospital for Sinners.*

[2] During the Reformation era, there was much debate between Protestants and Roman Catholics over the nature of the church. At the center of the controversy was this question: What are the marks of a true Church? Regarding the Reformers' view, Edmund Clowney observes: "Three marks were defined in distinguishing a true church of Christ: true preaching of the Word; proper observance of the sacraments; and faithful

number of SBC congregations that *do not* affirm the doctrines of grace but have, nevertheless, in recent years, shifted to an elder-led polity, *because they believe it is the biblical model*. So, this assertion appears to be just another attempt to stoke fear in the minds of those who are already suspicious of so-called "extreme" Calvinism.

(2) *It presents a false dichotomy*. The Bible supports neither a strict congregational model nor a strict elder-led model, but rather, a blending of the two. The New Testament model for church polity is known as *plural, elder-led congregationalism*. Let us unpack this term.

Plurality of Elders

The New Testament does not prescribe a particular form of church government, but the pattern we find there is clearly a plurality of elders. As Gregg Allison affirms: "Without exception, every time the New Testament mentions the government of a particular church, the leadership structure is a plurality of elders."[3] Consider, for example, the following New

exercise of church discipline." Edmund P. Clowney, *The Church*, Contours of Theology, ed. Gerald Bray (Downers Grove, IL: IVP, 1995), 101. It should be noted, however, that not all of the Reformers believed church discipline was an essential mark of a true church, though they did believe it was essential for the spiritual health and wellbeing of the church.

[3] Gregg R. Allison, *Sojourners and Strangers: The Doctrine of the Church* (Wheaton IL: Crossway, 2012), 293. Brian Croft affirms: "Although not explicitly stated by Paul to Timothy, it is consistently implied all through the New Testament that there is to be more than one pastor and deacon in the local church. Other than the passages that describe the qualifications of a

Testament texts: Acts 14:23; 15:4, 6, 22; 16:4; 20:17, 28; Philippians 1:1; 1 Timothy 5:17; Titus 1:5; James 5:14; 1 Peter 5:1.

According to Phil Newton and Matt Schmucker: "The term elder (*presbuteros*) and its cognates are found sixty-six times in the New Testament."[4]

Moreover, Tom Schreiner states:

> The word 'elder' is the most common term for leaders in the New Testament. How few know that the word 'pastor' (Eph. 4:11) only occurs once in the New Testament! Many Protestants who claim to be devoted to the Scriptures are often abysmally ignorant of what the Scriptures actually teach. We all too easily exalt human traditions over the Word of God.[5]

Schreiner, of course, is not insinuating that we should abandon the title "pastor."[6] Rather, his con-

---

pastor or deacon (1 Tim. 3:1–13; Titus 1:5–9) there are numerous examples of both these offices serving with other qualified men, sharing the responsibilities (Acts 20:28; 1 Pet. 5:1–4; Heb. 13:17). Not to mention, the burdens and responsibilities of these two offices are too great for one man to carry." Brian Croft, *Biblical Church Revitalization: Solutions for Dying & Divided Churches* (Ross-shire, UK: Christian Focus, 2016), 73–74.

[4] Phil A. Newton and Matt Schmucker, *Elders in the Life of the Church: Rediscovering the Biblical Model for Church Leadership* (Grand Rapids, MI: Kregal, 2014), 46.

[5] Thomas R. Schreiner, in the forward to Benjamin L. Merkle, *40 Questions About Elders and Deacons* (Grand Rapids, MI: Kregal, 2008), 12.

[6] Dever notes: "In the New Testament the words 'elder,' 'shepherd' or 'pastor,' and 'bishop' or 'overseer,' are used interchangeably." Mark Dever, *The Church: The Gospel Made Visible* (Nashville, TN: B&H, 2012), 54.

cern is that the local church be ordered according to the biblical pattern. Schriener continues:

> Jesus Christ is the head of the church, and we derive our instructions from Him. The church is not a human institution or idea. The ordering of the church is not a matter of our wisdom or preference. The church is not a business where the brightest executives brainstorm on how it should be organized. Too many conceive of the church as a human organism where we innovatively map out its structure. God has not left us to our own devices. He has given us instruction in His inspired and authoritative Word. To jettison what God says about the church and supplant it with our own ideas is nothing less than astonishing arrogance. As members of the church we do not give others our own wisdom, but what we have learned from Jesus Christ our Lord.[7]

Congregationalism

Congregationalism is a historic Baptist principle, which Southern Baptists believe to be rooted in Scripture. Allison defines it as follows:

> The term "congregationalism" indicates government by the (local) congregation. General-

---

[7] Schreiner, *40 Questions About Elders and Deacons*, 12.

ly speaking, congregationalism "rests authority of the church in each local congregation as an autonomous unit, with no person or organization above it except Christ the Head." This means that congregationalism diverges from both episcopalianism and its insistence on authoritative bishops above local churches, and presbyterianism with its structure of representative governing bodies (presbyteries/classes, synods, and/or general assemblies) above the local churches. Furthermore, congregationalism is based on two essential concepts: (1) autonomy, that is, the local church is independent and self-governing (it is responsible for its own finances, calls its own pastor, owns its own property and building, and the like); and (2) democracy, that is, the authority within the local church resides in its individual members, all of whom participate in congregational decisions through democratic processes. The Baptist Faith and Message affirms these two concepts in its definition of a church as "an autonomous local congregation of baptized believers ... [that] operates under the lordship of Christ through democratic processes. In such a congregation each member is responsible and accountable to Christ as Lord."[8]

---

[8] Allison, *Sojourners and Strangers*, 277. The quotes are by Robert L. Saucy, *The Churches in God's Program* (Chicago, IL: Moody Bible Institute, 1972), 114, and from the *Baptist Faith and Message*, VI, respectively.

Furthermore, the shape of congregationalism has varied in Baptist life throughout our history. As Allison further explains:

> Two main models that have historical precedent and find strong proponents today— indeed, a significant debate between proponents of these types is being carried out—are the single pastor–board of deacons model and the plurality of elders model. . . . Though the congregation is vested with authority to govern itself (without the intervention of bishops or governing structures above itself), a significant structure internal to the church also exercises authority to govern in the areas of responsibility delegated to it. This internal structure is either a single pastor–board of deacons, or a plurality of elders. . . . Despite . . . [the] various arguments in favor of the single pastor with plurality of deacons model of church government, the position and its support are not without their difficulties. A pattern of plurality of elders *is* established from the New Testament data; *all* the examples of churches found on its pages were led by a multiple group of pastors, and *no* church had a single elder.[9]

[9] Ibid., 287–290.

A Delicate Relationship

Nevertheless, the vast majority of Southern Baptists today object to a plural-eldership model.[10] This is mainly due to the fear of a misuse of authority. People hear the word "elders" and immediately think of power grabbers who do not allow the congregation to have a say in anything.[11] But this is not at all what we mean by *plural elder-led congregationalism*. John Hammett explains the term well when he asserts:

> The church has final authority over the elders, but the elders lead the congregation. . . . Congregationalism allows for *leadership* by pastors, elders, and/or deacons, even strong leadership and a measure of delegated authority. It does not allow for *government* by leaders. Congregationalism is *government* by the congregation.[12]

[10] Although not a universal practice among earlier Baptists, plural elder-led congregationalism was once the norm. See article by Mark Dever, "Baptists and Elders" [Originally delivered at the *Issues in Baptist Polity* Conference, hosted by The Baptist Center for Theology and Ministry at New Orleans Baptist Theological Seminary, February 6, 2004.]; available at http://sites.silaspartners.com/cc/article/0,,PTID314526_CHID598016_CIID144980,00.html.

[11] This can be true of *any* form of church polity. Many a Baptist church today identifies itself as "deacon-led," but in reality it is "deacon-*ran*"!

[12] John S. Hammett, *Biblical Foundations for Baptist Churches: A Contemporary Ecclesiology* (Grand Rapids, MI: Kregel, 2005), 145–146. It is important to note that Hammett is not saying that congregationalism is a pure democracy. Regarding this, Dayton Hartman argues: "In this model ... the congregation has the final authority—under the direction of the Scriptures—in matters of doctrine and church discipline. In its most biblically faithful form, a plurality of elders or pastors lead. However, some congregations, which misconstrue the biblical precedence for congregational rule,

Theoretically speaking, however, there is a delicate tension within the elder-congregation relationship. As Hammett further observes:

> On the one hand, church members are called upon to recognize their leaders' authority, submit to them, and obey them (see 1 Thess. 5:12; Heb. 13:17). . . . On the other hand, the way leaders exercise their authority in the New Testament is never dictatorial, but with a humble spirit, open to the input of others, and seeking to "lead the church into spiritually minded consensus."[13]

Although many modern Baptists are uncomfortable with the idea of pastoral authority, it is nevertheless established in the New Testament. As Strauch points out:

> Because the elders bear greater responsibility for the spiritual care of the entire congregation than other members, Scripture teaches that the congregation is to highly esteem, love, and honor its pastor elders (1 Thess.

practice a form of governance far more indebted to American democracy than to the Bible." Dayton Hartman, *Church History for Modern Ministry: Why Our Past Matters for Everything We Do* (Bellingham, WA: Lexham, 2016), 6.

[13] Hammett, *Biblical Foundations for Baptist Churches*, 165. Quote by D. A. Carson, "Church, Authority in the" in *Evangelical Dictionary of Theology*, ed. Walter A. Elwell, Second Edition (Grand Rapids, MI: Baker, 1999), 251.

5:12, 13; 1 Tim 5:17). Scripture also expressly
commands the congregation to obey and
submit to its spiritual leaders (Heb. 13:17).[14]

Clearly, the concept of pastoral authority is *biblical*
and therefore must not be rejected; but nor should
the terms "obey" and "submit" be exploited. Strauch
continues:

> The requirement to submit, however, is not
> meant to suggest blind, mindless submission.
> Nor does it suggest that elders are above
> questioning or immune from public discipline
> (1 Tim. 5:19ff.). The elders are most assuredly
> answerable to the congregation, and the con-
> gregation is responsible to hold its spiritual
> leaders accountable to faithful adherence to
> the truth of the Word. . . . All members have a
> voice in assuring that what is done in the
> church family is done according to Scripture.
> So there is a tightly knit, delicate, and recip-
> rocal relationship between elders and congre-
> gation.[15]

The Elder-Deacon Relationship

In most Southern Baptist churches today, the deacons serve in sort of a dual-role capacity (that is, as

[14] Alexander Strauch, *Biblical Eldership: An Urgent Call to Restore Biblical Church Leadership* (Littleton, CO: Lewis & Roth, 1995), 292.
[15] Ibid.

deacon-elders). But we must ask: *Is this the pattern we see in the New Testament?* In view of the biblical witness, the burden of proof lies with those who embrace a single-pastor-board-of-deacons model.

Moreover, many today are confused about the biblical roles assigned to deacons and elders. Strauch rightly notes: "In the New Testament, deacons are always associated with overseers, yet are subordinate to and distinct from them."[16] Strauch further maintains: "The two offices of overseers and servants, are meant to complement one another. One is the office of pastoral oversight; the other is the office of practical service to the needy."[17] This is an important distinction. When elders and deacons fulfill their biblically assigned roles, there is generally greater harmony among the leadership, the church's fellowship is blessed, and the ministry of the Word flourishes (Acts 6:1–7). However, as Croft asserts:

> When leadership fails to follow a biblical model a church cannot move towards church health. Church health, as well as a church for that matter, will rise and fall on its leaders,

[16] Alexander Strauch, *Minister of Mercy: The New Testament Deacon* (Littleton, CO: Lewis & Roth, 1992), 58.

[17] Ibid., 75. Likewise, Croft claims: "The office of a pastor is . . . referred to as 'an overseer' . . . A deacon's primary role is that of service. This is not to say that deacons do not oversee certain ministries, nor does this imply that pastors should not serve. But this refers to the primary biblical role of each office where the pastors exercise oversight (lead, oversee, administer) over all matters within the local church and the deacons lead in service, under the submission of the pastors" (*Biblical Church Revitalization*, 74).

their roles, and a church's willingness to follow them.[18]

Conclusion

Plural, elder-led congregationalism has been suc-
cinctly described as: Christ-*ruled*, elder-*led*, deacon-
served, and congregationally-*governed*. That is a
very accurate description. And, significantly, *this* is
the model we find in the pages of the New Testament!

[18] Ibid., 36–37. Mark Dever observes the following advantages of having
a plurality of elders: "Working together with [the] senior pastor, the plurality of elders aid both him and the church by rounding out the pastors gifts,
making up for his shortcomings, supplementing his judgment, and creating
support in the congregation for decisions, leaving leaders less exposed to
unjust criticism. A plurality also makes leadership more rooted and perma-
nent, and it allows for more mature continuity. It encourages the church to
take more responsibility for the spiritual growth of its own members and
helps make the church less dependent on its employees. As the elders lead
and the deacons serve, the congregation is prepared to live as the witness
God intends his church to be" (*The Church*, 59).

Bibliography

Allison, Gregg R. *Sojourners and Strangers: The Doctrine of the Church*. Wheaton IL: Crossway, 2012.

Ascol, Thomas K. "Charles Spurgeon and Courage in the Pulpit." Founders Ministries (March 16, 2017). Available at https://founders.org/2017/03/16charles-spurgeon-and-courage-in-the-pulpit/.

_____. *Traditional Theology & the SBC: An Interaction and Response to the Traditionalist Statement of God's Plan of Salvation*. Revised Edition. Cape Carol, FL: Founders Press, 2018.

Barrett, Matthew M. "A Scriptural Affirmation of Monergism." In *Whosoever He Wills: A Surprising Display of Sovereign Mercy*. Eds. Matthew Barrett and Thomas J. Nettles. Cape Coral, FL: Founders Ministries, 2012.

Benedict, David. *A General History of the Baptist Denomination in America*. New York, NY: Lewis Colby & Co., 1853.

Bennett, David. *The Altar Call: Its Origins and Present Usage*. Lanham, MD: University Press of America, 2000.

Blaire, Hugh J. "Antinomianism." In *New International Dictionary of the Christian Church*. Ed. J. D. Douglas. Grand Rapids, MI: Zondervan, 1974.

Boice, James Montgomery and Philip Graham Ryken. *The Doctrines of Grace: Rediscovering the Evangelical Gospel*. Wheaton, IL: Crossway Books, 2002.

Boykin, Samuel. *History of the Baptist Denomination in Georgia*. Atlanta, GA: The Christian Index, 1881.

Branham, I. R. "More Samples," *The Christian Index* (1 October 1891).

Calvin, John. *Commentary on a Harmony of the Evangelists, Matthew, Mark, and Luke*. Vol. 3. Trans. William Pringle. Grand

Rapids, MI: Baker, Reprinted Edition 2005.

_____. "Sermon on 1 Tim. 2:3–5." In *Calvin's Sermons: The Mystery of Godliness*. Grand Rapids, MI: Eerdmans, 1950.

Carson, D. A. "Church, Authority in the." In *Evangelical Dictionary of Theology*.

Second Edition. Ed. Walter A. Elwell. Grand Rapids, MI: Baker, 1999.

_____. *The Difficult Doctrine of the Love of God*. Wheaton, IL: Crossway, 2000.

_____. *Divine Sovereignty and Human Responsibility: Biblical Perspectives in Tension*. Grand Rapids, MI: Baker, 1994.

_____. *The Gospel According to John*. Grand Rapids, MI: Eerdmans, 1991. Chattahoochee Baptist Association. *Manuscript minutes*, 1871.

Clowney, Edmund P. *The Church*. In Contours of Theology. Ed. Gerald Bray. Downers Grove, IL: IVP, 1995.

Criswell, W. A. "The Effectual Calling of God." Sermon on Romans 9:15–16 delivered on Sunday morning at First Baptist Church in Dallas, TX (June 5, 1983). Available at https://www.wacriswell.com/sermons/1983/the-effectual-calling-of-god1/.

Croft, Brian. *Biblical Church Revitalization: Solutions for Dying & Divided Churches*. Ross-shire, UK: Christian Focus, 2016.

Custance, Arthur. *The Sovereignty of Grace*. Phillipsburg, NJ: P&R Publishing, 1979.

Dallimore, Arnold. *George Whitefield*. Vol. 1. Edinburgh, UK: Banner of Truth Trust, 1970.

Davis, Andy M. "Unconditional Election: A Biblical and God-Glorifying Doctrine." In *Whosoever He Wills: A Surprising Display of Sovereign Mercy*. Eds. Matthew Barrett and Tomas J. Nettles. Cape Coral, FL: Founders Ministries, 2012.

Dever, Mark. "Baptists and Elders." Presented at the *Issues in Baptist Polity* Conference, The Baptist Center for Theology and Ministry at New Orleans Baptist Theological Seminary (February 6, 2004). Available at http:// sites.silaspartners.com/cc/article/0,,PTID314526_CHID598016_CHID1744980,00.htm

_____. *The Church: The Gospel Made Visible*. Nashville, TN: B&H, 2012. DeYoung, Kevin. *Does Calvinism Kill Missions?* The Gospel Coalition (July 3, 2013). Available at https://www.thegospelcoalition.org/blogs/kevin-deyoung/does-calvinism-kill-missions/.

Edwards, Jonathan. "The Eternity of Hell Torments." In *The Torments of Hell: Jonathan Edwards on Eternal Damnation*. Ed. William C. Nichols.Ames, IA: International Outreach, 2006.

_____. *Treatise on Grace*. Ed. Paul Helm. Cambridge: James Clarke and Co., 1971.

Estep, William. "Calvinizing Southern Baptists." In *Texas Baptist Standard*, March 26, 1997.

Flint River Baptist Association. *Manuscript minutes*, 1829.

Gatiss, Lee. *For Us and For Our Salvation: 'Limited Atonement' in the Bible, Doctrine, History, and Ministry*. London, UK: The Latimer Trust, 2012.

Geisler, Norman L. *Chosen But Free: A Balanced View of God's Sovereignty and Free Will*. Third Edition. Bloomington, MN: Bethany House Publishers, 2010.

George, Timothy. *Amazing Grace: God's Pursuit, Our Response*. Second Edition. Wheaton, IL: Crossway, 2011.

_____. *Baptist Confessions, Covenants, and Catechisms*. Eds. Timothy and Denise George. Nashville, TN: Broadman and Holman, 1996.

Gerstner, John R. *Atonement*. Ed. Gabriel N. E. Fluhrer. Phillipsburg, NJ: P&R Publishing, 2010.

Hammett, John S. *Biblical Foundations for Baptist Churches: A Contemporary Ecclesiology*. Grand Rapids, MI: Kregel, 2005.

_____. "The Why and Who of Church Membership." In *Baptist Foundations: Church Government for an Anti-Institutional Age*. Eds. Mark Dever and Jonathan Leeman. Nashville, TN: B&H, 2015.

Hartman, Dayton. *Church History for Modern Ministry: Why Our Past Matters for Everything We Do*. Bellingham, WA: Lexham, 2016.

The History Committee Sarepta Baptist Association. *Minutes of the Sarepta Baptist Association For the Years of 1799 Through 1849*. Restored from the Micro-Film of Minutes and from the printed Minutes for these years. Athens, GA: Sarepta Baptist Association, 2002.

Horton, Michael. *For Calvinism*. Grand Rapids, MI: Zondervan, 2011.

Kidd, Thomas. "A Brief History of the Altar Call." The Gospel Coalition (July 24, 2017). Available at https://www.thegospel coalition.org/blogs/evangelical-history/a-brief-history-of-the-altar-call/.

Kostenberger, Andreas J. *John*. In Baker Exegetical Commentary on the New Testament. Grand Rapids, MI: Baker Academic, 2004.

Land, Richard. "Congruent Election: Understanding Election from an 'Eternal Now' Perspective." In *Whosoever Will: A Biblical-Theological Critique of Five-Point Calvinism*. Eds. David L. Allen and Steven W. Lemke. Nashville, TN: B&H, 2010.

Leeman, Jonathan. "You Asked: Should Churches Perform Altar Calls?" The Gospel Coalition (November 16, 2011). Available at https://www.thegospelcoalition.org/article/you-asked-should-churches-perform-altar-calls/.

Lloyd-Jones, D. Martyn. "Dr. Lloyd-Jones on the Altar Call." Banner of Truth (June 21, 2003). Available at https://banneroftruth.org/us/resources/ srticles/2003/ dr-lloyd-jones-on-the-altar-call/.

Long, Gary D. *Definite Atonement*. CreateSpace Independent Publishing Platform, November 14, 2014.

Marshall, I. Howard. *Kept By the Power of God: A Study of Perseverance and Falling Away*. London, UK: Epworth Press, 1969.

_____. "Universal Grace and Atonement in the Pastoral Epistles." In *A Case for Arminianism*. Grand Rapids, MI: Zondervan Publishing House, 1989.

Moo, Douglas J. *Romans*. In The NIV Zondervan Study Bible. Ed. D. A. Carson. Grand Rapids, MI: Zondervan, 2015.

Morris, Leon. *The Gospel According to John*. In The New International Commentary on the New Testament. Grand Rapids, MI: Eerdmans, 1971.

Murray, Iain H. *The Forgotten Spurgeon*. Reset Edition. Carlisle, PA: The Banner of Truth Trust, 2009.

_____. *The Invitation System*. Carlisle, PA: The Banner of Truth Trust, 2002.

Murray, John. *Redemption Accomplished and Applied*. Grand Rapids, MI: Eerdmans, 1955.

Murrell, Adam. *Predestined to Believe: Common Objections to the Reformed Faith Answered*. Second Edition. Eugene, OR: Resource Publications.

Nettles, Thomas J. *Baptist Catechisms*. Ed. Thomas J. Nettles. Memphis, TN: Mid-America Baptist Seminary.

_____. *By His Grace and for His Glory: A Historical, Theological and Practical Study of the Doctrines of Grace in Baptist Life*. Revised and Expanded 20th Anniversary Edition. Cape Coral, FL: Founders Press, 2006.

Newton, John. *The Works of the Rev. John Newton*. Edinburgh, UK: Thomas Nelson, 1849.

Newton, Phil A. and Matt Schmucker. *Elders in the Life of the Church: Rediscovering the Biblical Model for Church Leadership*. Grand Rapids, MI: Kregal, 2014

Nichols, Stephen J. *Jonathan Edwards: A Guided Tour of his Life and Thought*. Phillipsburg, NJ: P&R Publishing, 2001.

Orrick, Jim Scott. *Mere Calvinism*. Phillipsburg, NJ: P&R Publishing, 2019. Owen, John. "The Death of Death in the Death of Christ." In *Works of John Owen*. Edinburg: Banner of Truth Trust, 1966.

Packer, J. I. *Evangelism and the Sovereignty of God*. Downers Grove, IL: InterVarsity Press, 1961.

_____. "The Love of God: Universal and Particular." In *Still Sovereign: Contemporary Perspectives on Election, Foreknowledge, & Grace.* Grand Rapids, MI: Baker, 2000.

_____. *The Quest for Godliness*. Wheaton, IL: Crossway, 1994.

Page, Frank S. *Trouble with the Tulip: A Closer Examination of the Five Points of Calvinism*. Second Edition. Canton, GA: Riverstone Group, 2006.

Palmer, Edwin H. *The Person and Ministry of the Holy Spirit: The Traditional Calvinist Perspective*. Grand Rapids, MI: Baker, 1974.

Peterson, Robert A. *Election and Free Will: God's Gracious Choice and Our Responsibility*. In Explorations of Biblical Theology Series. Ed. Robert A. Peterson. Phillipsburg, NJ: P&R Publishing, 2007.

_____. *Our Secure Salvation: Preservation and Apostasy*. In Explorations of Biblical Theology Series. Ed. Robert A. Peterson. Phillipsburg, NJ: P&R Publishing, 2009.

Piper, John. *Five Points: Towards a Deeper Experience of God's Grace*. Ross- shire, UK: Christian Focus, 2013.

_____. *Let the Nations Be Glad! The Supremacy of God in Missions*. Third Edition. Grand Rapids, MI: Baker Academic, 2010.

_____. *The Pleasures of God: Meditations on God's Delight in Being God*. Colorado Springs, CO: Multnomah Books, 2000.

Platt, David. "Divine Sovereignty: The Fuel of Death-Defying Missions." Session VI. Together For The Gospel, 2012. Available at https://t4g.org/media/2012/05/divine-sovereignty-the-fuel-of-dea

th-defying-missions-2/.

Reid, W. S. "Reprobation." In *Evangelical Dictionary of Theology*. Second Edition. Ed. Walter A. Elwell. Grand Rapids, MI: Baker, 1999.

Reisinger, Ernest C. Publisher's Introduction to J. P. Boyce's *Abstract of Systematic Theology*. Reprinted Edition. Pompano Beach, FL: Christian Gospel Foundation, original copy 1887.

Rose, Nathan. "On Altar Calls and Invitations." (North American Missions Board, SBC, Replant Blog 2018). Available at https://www.namb.net/replant-blog/on-altar-calls-and-invitations/.

Schreiner, Thomas R. *Commentary on Hebrews*. In Biblical Theology for Christian Proclamation. Eds. T. Desmond Alexander, Andreas J. Kostenberger and Thomas R. Schreiner. Nashville, TN: B&H Publishing Group, 2015.

_____. "Effectual Call and Grace." In *Still Sovereign: Contemporary Perspectives on Election, Foreknowledge, & Grace*. Grand Rapids, MI: Baker Books, 2000.

_____. Forward to Benjamin L. Merkle. *40 Questions About Elders and Deacons*. Grand Rapids, MI: Kregal, 2008.

_____. *Romans*. In Baker Exegetical Commentary on the New Testament. Ed. Moisés Silva. Grand Rapids, MI: Baker Academic, 1998.

Schrock, David. "Jesus Saves, No Asterisk Needed." In *Whosoever He Wills: A Surprising Display of Sovereign Mercy*. Eds. Matthew Barrett and Thomas J. Nettles. Cape Coral, FL: Founders Ministries, 2012.

Selph, Robert B. *Southern Baptists and the Doctrine of Election*. Harrisonburg, VA: Sprinkle Publications, 1988.

Smith, Brandon and Kurt Smith. *The Gospel Heritage of Georgia Baptists:1772–1830*. Birmingham, AL: Solid Ground Christian Books, 2016.

Sproul, R. C. *Chosen By God*. Carol Stream, IL: Tyndale House, 1986.

_____. *Everyone's A Theologian: An Introduction to Systematic Theology*. Sanford, FL: Reformation Trust, 2014.

_____. *What Is Reformed Theology? Understanding the Basics*. Grand Rapids, MI: Baker Books, 1997.

Sarepta Baptist Association. *Manuscript minutes*, 1830. Spurgeon, C. H. "Divine Sovereignty" (Sermon # 77, Vol. 2).

_____. "Effects of Sound Doctrine." Sermon delivered on Sunday evening, April 22, 1860, at New Park Street Chapel.

_____. *Metropolitan Tabernacle Pulpit*. Vol. XVI. Pasadena, TX: Pilgrim Publications, 1981.

_____. *Metropolitan Tabernacle Pulpit*, Vol. XV. Pasadena, TX: Pilgrim Publications, 1984.

_____. *New Park Street Pulpit*. Vol. V. Pasadena, TX: Pilgrim Publications, 1981.

_____. "Particular Redemption" (Sermon # 181).

Steele, David N., Curtis C. Thomas and S. Lance Quinn. *The Five Points of Calvinism: Defined, Defended, and Documented*. Updated and Expanded. Phillipsburg, NJ: P&R Publishing, 2004.

Stewart, Kenneth J. *Ten Myths About Calvinism: Rediscovering the Breadth of the Reformed Tradition*. Downers Grove, IL: InterVarsity, 2011.

Stillwell, J. M. "Social Circle, Stone Mountain, Indian Creek." *The Christian Index* (27 November 1873).

Stott, John R. W. *Romans: God's Good News for the World*. Downers Grove, IL: InterVarsity, 1994.

Strauch, Alexander. *Biblical Eldership: An Urgent Call to Restore Biblical Church Leadership*. Littleton, CO: Lewis & Roth, 1995.

_____. *Minister of Mercy: The New Testament Deacon*. Littleton, CO: Lewis & Roth, 1992.

Thorn, Joe. "The Problem of 'Angry Calvinists.'" Justin Taylor (September 16, 2011). Available at https://www.thegospelcoali tion.org/blogs/justin-taylor/the-problem-of-angry-calvinists/.

Tugalo Baptist Association. *Manuscript minutes*, 1824.

_____. *Manuscript minutes*, 1831.

Westcott, B. F. *The Gospel According to St John: The Greek Text with Introduction and Notes*. Vol. 1, 124.

Western Baptist Association. *Manuscript minutes*, 1833.

White, James R. *The Potter's Freedom: A Defense of the Reformation and a Rebuttal of Norman Geisler's Chosen But Free*. Amityville, NY: Calvary Press Publishing, 2000.

Wills, Gregory. *Democratic Religion: Freedom, Authority, and Church Discipline in the Baptist South 1785-1900*. New York, NY: Oxford, 1997.